How *to* WIN *at* GARDENING

How *to* WIN *at* GARDENING

A PRACTICAL A-TO-Z GUIDE TO A BETTER GARDEN

RICHARD JACKSON
and
CAROLYN HUTCHINSON

Reader's Digest

Acknowledgments

The publishers thank the following for their kind permission to
reproduce the photographs in this book:

David Austin Roses Ltd page 101; **Gillian Beckett** pages 27, 38 (top), 63 (top), 65 (top),
73 (top right), 101 (bottom), 109 (top left); **Deni Bown** pages 71, 73 (top left), 74;
Crown copyright Brogdale pages37 (top), 40 (top); **The Garden Picture Library**
pages 1 (J. Sira), 52 (Clive Nichols), 55 and 57 (bottom) (John Glover), 58 (top) (Bob
Challoner); **Bob Gibbons Natural Image** pages 24, 97, 98, 103 (bottom), 105, 108, 109
(top right), 122, 131 (top), 134 (top middle and right), 135, 136, 137, 138, 139;
John Glover Photography pages 8, 22, 42, 43, 44, 45, 96, 100;
Harkness New Roses page 102 (bottom); **Holt Studios** pages 88, 89, 90, 92,
93 (bottom), 94 (bottom right); **Levingtons/Fisons Horticultural Ltd** page 35 (bottom);
Mattocks Roses of Oxford page 102 (top); **Ken Muir** pages 38 (bottom), 39, 40 (bottom),
41; **Photos Horticultural Picture Library** pages 6, 26 (bottom), 36, 59 (bottom), 76, 79,
82, 84, 85, 87, 102, 103 (top), 104, 107 (top), 116, 119, 120 (top), 121, 122, 123, 124;
Stapeley Water Gardens Ltd, Cheshire pages 133 (bottom), 134 (top left);
Graham Strong, Garden Folio page s 35 (top), 56, 57 (top right), 66, 120 (bottom),
125, 133 (top), 140, 142 (right), 144, 154, 155; **Suttons Group of Companies Ltd,
Torquay, Devon** pages 9, 10 (top), 14, 15 (bottom), 37, 50, 58 (bottom), 59 (top right);
Thompson & Morgan Seeds Ltd, (UK)
page 59 (top left); **Valley Green (UK)** page 64.

All other photographs supplied by *Garden Answers* magazine .

A Reader's Digest Book
Edited and produced by HarperCollins*Publishers*
Editorial Director: *Polly Powell*
Editor: *Becky Humphreys*

First published in Great Britain 1996
U.S. edition published 1998

ISBN 0-7621-0007-9
Library of Congress Cataloging in Publication Data has been applied for.

Printed in Italy

Contents

Introduction

This practical and inspiring book arms gardeners with the knowledge to succeed. Practical advice, based on the real experience of the authors and presented in a lively but informative style, gives the new gardener in particular the confidence to give it a shot, while providing inspiration for enthusiasts to try something new. The book covers all aspects of gardening that interest today's gardeners — from growing plants in containers to ideas for low maintenance — without dwelling too long on traditional, time-consuming techniques that have lost favor with busy gardeners. Packed with planting ideas and expert tips, it shows how to achieve results quickly and easily. The authors deal with problem solving in a down-to-earth manner, so that keeping weeds in check and pests and diseases at bay can be seen as simple routine rather than a difficult chore. With its recommended plant varieties and practical suggestions for making the most of everything, from roses to hanging baskets, this book provides readers with all they need to know to become expert gardeners!

Bedding plants

You just can't beat bedding plants for sheer flower power. Whether planted in mass drifts, like the popular park bedding schemes of old, or used selectively in small groups, they give a wonderful display for months on end.

Most bedding plants are annuals, lasting only one season, but tender perennials like geraniums and fuchsias can live for years if you baby them a bit indoors during the winter.

There's only one problem: bedding plants can be hard work. To keep them looking their best, they need regular watering, feeding, and deadheading. But millions of gardeners know that if you can spare the time, it's well worth the effort for such glorious results.

Sturdy, healthy plug-grown plants are great value for the money.

GROWING SUCCESS

Bedding plants can be grown from seed, and it's certainly the cheapest method, but for gardening beginners it's much simpler to buy them as transplants, which are available at various stages of growth.

Seedlings are supplied in small pots or boxes, each densely sown with around 100 plants. These should be carefully separated (pricked out) and transplanted to seed trays or individual pots of good compost; handle them by the leaves and take care not to damage roots or stems. In seed trays, space the seedlings at 2 in/5cm intervals so that they have room to grow. Give them a sunny location on a windowsill or in a frost-free greenhouse and keep them evenly watered; they should be ready to plant out by late spring.

Small plug-grown plants are individually grown in miniature cells of compost, and it's very easy to pop them out of the cells, transfer them to individual 3½ in/9cm pots; and grow them indoors before planting them out. There's minimal root disturbance, and they should develop rapidly. Plugs are particularly good value, and there's an excellent range to choose from. Seedlings and plugs are available from early spring, but by midspring, you should find a tempting selection of annuals ready to plant out as soon as possible after the last frost in your area (see Hardiness Zone Map, page 156). These more mature plants are sold in flats, market paks, and pots.

Of the three, flats are usually the cheapest, but the plants are small and will take a while longer to establish after planting, especially as

PLANTING IN THE GARDEN

To get your plants off to a flying start, it's worth improving the soil by adding some organic matter, like compost, before planting. It's not essential, but if you fork in 2–3 in/ 5–7.5cm to the surface, it will really give them a boost.

Water the soil if it's a bit dry, and soak the plants an hour or so before taking them out of their containers.

Space them out (remembering their eventual spread), then dig the planting holes, each of which should be large enough to take the rootball comfortably at the same level as it was in the pot or market pak. Fill in around the rootball, gently firming the soil down. Finally, water the plants in and keep watering regularly until they have put out new roots and are growing well.

'Surfinia' petunias are astonishingly vigorous and free-flowering forms of this bedding favorite.

PLANTING IN POTS

Like most container plants, annuals hate to be waterlogged, so check that your pot has drainage holes, then add a layer of stones, pieces of broken clay pots, or foam packing "peanuts" to the bottom of the pot to allow better drainage. Add some potting mix; then plant your plants in exactly the same way you did in the garden. To conserve moisture and minimize watering chores, top the exposed soil with a thin layer of pebbles or an organic mulch.

AFTERCARE

Summer annuals need some tender loving care to get the most from them. Regular watering is essential, especially in the early stages when the plants are establishing a root system. In the absence of plentiful rain, a deep, thorough watering, twice a week, may be sufficient for plants in the ground, but those in containers will need a daily soaking if the weather is really hot and dry. Early evening is the best time for this, as less water will evaporate from the soil in cooler night temperatures. But be sure to water only the soil – not the foliage. Leaves and stems that remain wet overnight are vulnerable to diseases.

It's also vital to feed regularly – this helps produce healthier plants and lots more flowers, so it's well worth

Young plants ready to be potted.

root damage is inevitable when you're splitting them up. Potted plants are the most mature of all, and hence the most expensive, so you might like to compromise by using boxed cell-grown annuals. These have proved extremely popular over the past few years, with plants at an intermediate stage between flats and pots. The plants are easy to pop out of the cells and can be planted without any check in growth.

When choosing your annuals, avoid any that are dry (they'll feel very light as you pick them up) or potbound (with a mass of roots at the base), and certainly don't buy anything that's tall and spindly or has discolored leaves. Healthy, sturdy, bushy plants are going to perform far better in your garden.

PATIO-PACKS

Trailing Fuchsia
This pack contains 6 varieties for baskets, pots or planters

Suggested Care
Plant into 3" pots using new potting compost. Water and feed weekly. Pinch out top 1" after 10-14 days to encourage bushy growth. Transplant into hanging basket once established.

A beautiful garden all summer long.

Making the most of Geraniums

Geraniums are just about the easiest of all plants to grow as long as you give them a sunny location in well-drained soil. Officially, they should be called pelargoniums, to distinguish them from the true geraniums, which are hardy outdoor perennials. They were classified as pelargoniums 200-odd years ago, but it's taking us a while to get used to the idea.

There's a tremendous choice of more than 1,000 varieties, in upright and trailing forms. Flower colors range from deep red to pure white, and some cultivars even have variegated leaves. There is also a range of flower-head shapes – from big, globelike pompons to more open clusters.

The most free flowering are the seed-raised 'Multibloom' varieties, closely followed by the zonal types (those with rounded leaves that often bear a maroon horseshoe marking). Ivy-leaved trailing geraniums, which look so good in large pots and window boxes, are also very reliable. Martha Washington geraniums (with serrated edges to the leaves)

have the showiest flowers, but a much shorter flowering period.

TAKING CUTTINGS

If you want to increase your stocks, geraniums root incredibly easily from cuttings and mid-summer is the best time to take them. Choose a healthy plant and, using a sharp knife, cut off a strong shoot about 4 in/10cm long, just below a leaf joint. Trim off the lower leaves and any flowers or flower buds. Insert the cutting to a depth of 1 in/2.5cm or so, in a pot of dampened seed or potting mix; a 4 in/10cm pot will take up to five cuttings. Keep them on a light (not sunny) windowsill indoors, watering sparingly when the soil mix begins to dry, and they should root within three or four weeks (give a gentle tug to check). They can then be potted into individual $3^1/2$ in/9cm pots and left to develop further.

OVERWINTERING

Geraniums aren't winter hardy, so if you want to keep your plants from year to year, you must bring the pots indoors before the first frost. If they're planted in the ground, lift them with a hand fork, trying not to

Colorful geraniums adorn a window box.

break off too many roots, and transfer them to pots that are only a little larger than the rootball, filling in any gaps with potting mix.

Leggy plants can be cut back by as much as half but smaller plants don't need any pruning at all. Stand the pots in a cool, light spot indoors, water very infrequently so that the soil is barely moist, and remove any dead leaves. Don't worry if they continue flowering – leave them to it and enjoy the extra color. In spring, cut back any woody stems, water more frequently, and start to feed. Pinch out the tips of new shoots to encourage good bushy growth and repot if they're growing vigorously; when there's no longer any danger of frost, they can be safely set outdoors.

Geraniums are among the most reliable summer performers.

Making the most of Fuchsias

Mostly grown as container plants, there are hundreds of different fuchsias in a wonderful range of colors. Some trail, while others make superb bushes, and most spectacular of all are the tree-shaped "standards", trained on a single tall stem for accent plants. The dangling flowers, especially in the double forms, are very elegant and look particularly lovely against a haze of white or blue trailing lobelia.

Fuchsias dislike hot scorching sun and are happiest in slightly shaded spots. Morning sun is fine; it's the really hot afternoon blaze that can cause problems. They also hate getting too dry, so always keep the soil moist.

TAKING CUTTINGS

Taking cuttings is not only easy, it's a good investment, since fuchsias are quite expensive. The procedure is exactly the same as for geraniums, except that newly potted cuttings should be kept in a shady spot. Once they begin to grow strongly, move them to a lighter location and pinch out the tip of the main stem in order to encourage side shoots. In a few weeks, these side shoots will themselves need pinching out in order to develop a good bushy plant.

OVERWINTERING

Unlike their hardier garden cousins (which have smaller flowers), bedding fuchsias are tender and need protection from winter weather. But overwintering them is quite easy and it's well worth the effort. Bring them indoors when frost threatens, potting them up like geraniums. They need a resting period over winter, so keep them in a cool spot and remove the leaves as they die off. Water very infrequently, just to stop them from getting bone dry.

In spring, encourage them into active growth by first removing them from their pots, shaking off any loose soil, and repotting them in fresh potting mix. They can be cut back to around 2 in/5cm from the base (or, in the case of standard fuchsias, cut the head back to 2 in/5cm from the stem). Keep the soil moist and spray the wood occasionally with tepid water to get them growing. Once they're growing vigorously, pinch out the growing tips to encourage bushiness and water and feed regularly. Plant out when all danger of frost has passed.

Trailing fuchsias look their best on a garden table or low wall rather than at ground level.

Fuchsias bear elegant dangling blooms.

the effort. A once-weekly feeding of high-potassium fertilizer (liquid tomato food is excellent and relatively cheap) will really pay off for both garden and container plants – in our experience, it can help double the number of flowers produced. Delay feeding container plants for five or six weeks, when they will have used up all the plant foods in the fresh soil mix.

The other weekly chore is deadheading which some people actually enjoy. Unfortunately, most varieties will do their utmost to produce seed – this diverts the plant's energy from flower to seed production, and it will, after a while, virtually stop flowering. So as soon as you notice fading blooms, pinch them off at the base of the stalk; not only will this tidy up the plant, but it's your insurance policy for bountiful production of flowers in the coming weeks.

Spring-flowering bedding plants (like pansies, primroses, and forget-me-nots) are much easier to look after. They're generally planted as transplants in spring (or fall in mild winter climates) and need only the occasional watering if the weather is unusually dry. Then as it warms up, be sure to keep them moist and feed every two weeks through the season. And, of course, they will need regular deadheading.

COLOR AND SCENT

Although it's a matter of personal taste, some color combinations seem to work while others clash dreadfully. As a rule, try to avoid planting mixed colors of different bedding plants together. A mixture of one variety usually looks far better planted with a single color of another – pastel mixed impatiens with silver-leaved helichrysum, for instance, or white petunias as a soothing foreground for mixed geraniums.

You could, of course, keep it really simple and restrict yourself to just two or three colors. Pale blue, soft pink, and white are always effective together, or you could try a really eye-popping scheme of scarlet and purple. And if you have a really good color sense, try putting two or three shades of, say, blue together – very brave and, at the moment, very fashionable.

Make the most of winter and spring color, too. In early fall, garden centers have a good ready-to-plant selection, including wallflowers, pansies, polyanthus, and forget-me-nots. Winter-flowering pansies will in fact span both seasons, in milder climates, producing large, bright flowers right through the bleakest months, with a final burst of growth in spring. They look wonderful in containers and hanging baskets, as well as in the garden, where they should be planted in groups of one color where they can be seen and admired from the windows. In this way you don't have to venture outside to be able to enjoy their cheerful winter display.

Many bedding plants are sweetly scented, so place them close to doors and windows where you can enjoy their fragrance, which is usually best in the evening. Verbenas are good, and blue or purple petunias can smell as rich as any lily. Best of all, though, are 'Sensation' flowering tobacco plants (nicotiana), which will fill the air with their exquisite fragrance over a very wide area.

This garden offers a lovely color combination of white, soft purples, and silver.

Top Ten Bedding Plants

✦ SWEET ALYSSUM

One of the most popular, but slightly old-fashioned edging plants, producing sweetly scented flowers from late spring to fall. Although white is the usual choice, you can find them in rose pink, purple, and even apricot. Best in sun and a not too heavy soil. In hot summers it is prone to mildew and will stop flowering early. A good garden plant but not the best for hanging baskets, where it struggles to compete with other plants. Height 4 in/10cm.

✦ BEGONIA

Colorful and reliable plants for edging, beds, hanging baskets, and containers. They're drought resistant, and thrive in part sun or shade their

---

TIPS

Buy plants that have not yet started to bloom. If the plant has buds or flowers, pinch them out with your fingers after planting – this will ensure a bushier plant and more flowers over time.

Some bedding plants are labeled as F1 hybrids. These varieties have been specially bred to be more vigorous and uniform in size, habit, and color. But take note: these hybrids cannot be grown from seed. If you like a particular variety, you must buy new plants the following year.

When you're planting annuals in the garden, give the plants a treat by watering them in with liquid tomato food diluted to half strength – it really does get them growing more quickly.

---

only dislike is waterlogged soil. There are two main types. Fibrous-rooted (semperflorens) begonias grow 6 in/15cm high with attractive bronze or bright green leaves; the pretty flowers are usually red, pink, or white. Tuberous varieties are taller (12 in/30cm), with larger flowers in a wider range of vibrant colors. These are mostly used for container displays and can be lifted and stored indoors at the end of the season and then regrown the following year.

✦ IMPATIENS

A great favorite. Superb anywhere in the garden and in containers and hanging baskets. Flowers prolifically from a young age all summer (whatever the weather). Happy in part sun but also one of the best for shady spots. A compact plant at 10 in/25cm, it's available in more than 20 different colors. New Guinea hybrids are larger (18 in/45cm) and combine attractively colored leaves with terrific flower power; best grown in sun, they look particularly good in containers and can be overwintered indoors, treated like geraniums.

✦ LOBELIA

Sold in bush and trailing forms, lobelia can flower from late spring until fall, as long as the soil doesn't get too dry. It grows best in a fertile soil and sunny location. Both bush and trailing forms are available in white and red as well as the traditional shades of blue. Many gardeners find that the trailing forms become too straggly in hanging baskets, and they prefer to use the bushy types. Not recommended for hot regions.

Lobelia

✦ MARGUERITE DAISY (*Argyranthemum*)

A few years ago, the only marguerite widely available was the lovely white-flowered Paris daisy. But recently other, very pretty colors, including yellow and pink, have been introduced, and marguerites are now fashionable plants for containers and borders. They are easy to grow in most soils and prefer a sunny location. As tender perennials, they should be brought in for winter and treated like fuchsias. It's also very easy to root them from cuttings in summer.

✦ MARIGOLD (*Tagetes*)

Anyone can grow them, they flower quickly, and whatever variety you've chosen, the display will be bright and long lasting. There are four basic groups. African marigolds are generally taller, with large ball-like flowers, while their cousins, the French marigolds, are shorter and more spreading, with smaller flowers but in larger quantities. Just to confuse us, there is also a group called Afro-French marigolds, combining the dwarfness of the French with the huge double flowers of the Africans. Finally, there's the daintiest of the group, the plants we usually call signet marigolds, with fine feathery foliage and small single flowers. All are best in sun, in reasonable soil. And all bloom in very bright colors.

✦ PANSY (*Viola*)

Pansies really cannot be beat for a magnificent and reliable display of spring color. Some varieties (like 'Ultima' and 'Universal') flower during the winter as well, although they still peak in spring. The color range is enormous, from pure white to jet black, and pansies look good anywhere, whether in mixed colors in containers and hanging baskets or in groups of single colors in the border. Good in part sun, but especially useful in shade during the spring. For best results, deadhead regularly and water well in dry weather.

✦ PETUNIA

Magnificent plants for sunny spots in borders or containers. Happiest in hot summers, but the newer 'Multiflora' varieties are far more tolerant of wet weather. Don't grow petunias in moist, shady spots – they'll produce plenty of leaves but very few flowers. Available in lots of colors and in single and (less desirable, we think) double forms. 'Surfinia' varieties are spectacular in hanging baskets, flowering prolifically and growing up to ten times the size of traditional varieties. Neatest of all is the new 'Fantasy' series, with masses of small flowers on compact, bushy plants.

✦ PRIMROSES

Wonderful spring-flowering plants that look like English primroses but carry their flowers on short stalks. They are also much tougher than most hybrid primroses, which garden centers generally sell as indoor plants for cool rooms. Good in containers with dwarf tulips or daffodils, otherwise make a fine front-of-border plant. Best in moist soil in partial shade, flowering from early to late spring. Move them immediately after flowering to a shady spot in the garden, to make way for summer bedding.

✦ FLOWERING TOBACCO (*Nicotiana*)

There have been tremendous improvements in breeding over the past few years. The new introductions are superb, compact plants, the flowers staying open all

Flowering tobacco

day long. These are ideal, undemanding plants for borders and containers and they flower for months (early summer through fall). Sadly some of these new varieties, such as the excellent 'Domino' series (12 in/90cm), have lost the traditional scent, but garden centers still sell the taller growing 'Sensation' hybrids (36 in/90cm), which are fragrant. Flowering tobacco loves a good, well-drained soil in a sunny spot.

IDEAS FOR LOW-MAINTENANCE

When planting in the garden, create a slight saucer-shaped dip around each plant. This channels water straight to the rootball and saves both time and water because you can quickly direct the water to the specific plants, rather than watering the whole patch.

In a newly planted garden, use bedding plants to fill the gaps between immature shrubs and herbaceous plants. Not only will they look cheerful, but they'll keep the weeds down at the same time.

Marigold

Bulbs

Alliums

Bulbs are one of nature's best tricks: they are little time bombs, packed with all that's needed for a glorious explosion of flowers. All you need do is plant them and wait – the rest happens automatically.

To be pedantic for a moment, some bulbs are technically corms (crocus, for instance), and some are tubers (dahlias), but since they're all to be found in the same section at the garden center, let's not quibble. The great time for bulbs is the spring, with daffodils and tulips as the stars. But the show goes on year-round, from winter snowdrops to exotic summer lilies, so make the most of these easy-to-grow plants.

GROWING SUCCESS

Bulbs are undemanding plants, and very long-lived, but you can help them be their beautiful best by following a few ground rules.

First, pick out firm, plump bulbs, the bigger the better (more flower power). Reject any that are soft, mildewed, or sprouting. It's also important to check the packet to see that they have been commercially grown, rather than collected from the wild.

Then plant them as soon as possible – bulbs deteriorate if kept hanging around, especially in a warm room. The only bulb you should delay in planting is the tulip; they're available from August, but it's best to keep them in cool, dry conditions and plant in October. This stops them from coming up too early in spring and being harmed by any late hard frosts.

Planting at the correct depth is vital for success with bulbs, so check the recommended depth on the packet and stick to it. If you don't, the bulb will repay you by failing to flower. As a rule of thumb, if you've no packet information to guide you, bulbs should be planted at three times their own depth. Thus a 2 in/5cm bulb will need a 6 in/15cm deep hole. Make sure you plant them with their "noses" (the pointy end) facing up, but most will cope if you get it wrong.

In the garden, especially in hard ground, bulb

TWO-TIER PLANTING

Spring bulbs are naturals for containers, and in larger pots and tubs you can double their impact by planting in tiers. It's really quite simple: using a single cultivar of daffodil or tulip, follow our guide to planting in containers but set the first layer of bulbs at four times their own depth, leaving a bulb's-width between them. Cover with soil so that you can just see the "noses." Then place the second layer at the normal depth, so that they sit between the noses rather than on top of them, and fill in with more soil. The magic of this system is that, although the bulbs are at different depths, they will all flower at the same time, making a magnificent display.

A variation on this theme, if you're feeling adventurous, is to use bulbs that flower in succession. One of the best and simplest recipes is to plant tulips in a circle, then use the central area for early crocuses. The crocuses will give the first show, in early spring, with the tulips taking over later.

Tulips, daffodils, and Anemone blanda *flower brightly at the base of a tree.*

Making the most of Indoor Bulbs

AMARYLLIS (*Hippeastrum*)
The amaryllis, with its great strap-shaped leaves and huge trumpet flowers, is the most spectacular of all indoor bulbs and easy to grow.

If you buy yours as a dry bulb, choose the biggest one you can find and pot it up in potting mix, leaving the top third of the bulb exposed. This is a plant that actually prefers cramped conditions, so make sure that there is only 1 in/2.5cm or so of soil between the bulb and the pot. Place the pot in a warm, light spot and keep just moist until growth appears, then water more regularly and feed weekly with liquid tomato food or indoor plant fertilizer.

Amaryllis often keep their leaves right through the year, but sometimes they decide they want a rest. So if the leaves yellow and die back, just stop watering and keep it dry for two or three months. Gentle watering will then stimulate growth. Repot every two or three years.

HYACINTHS FOR CHRISTMAS

Hyacinths are available in garden centers from August onwards, and it's essential, if you want your specimen to flower for Christmas, that you plant them by early September and give them a chilling period.

If you're using a bulb bowl or any other container without drainage holes, the best soil mix is coarse peat moss with crushed oyster shell and charcoal, which stays moist without compacting, but a well-drained potting mix will suffice. Fill the bowl with soil, then set in the bulbs so that they're almost touching, with their noses just showing. Water gently so that the soil is moist but not sodden.

Now set the bowl in a dark, cool spot and water only as necessary. Once the leaves have emerged and you can just see the flower spike, move the bowl into a position that gets more light and let the plants grow. As soon as the flower buds are ready to open, just bring the plant into a warm room where they will very quickly develop fully and fill it with their unique perfume.

NARCISSI (*Paperwhites*)
At the garden center you'll find a small section devoted to indoor varieties of narcissus. Most of them have a marvelous scent and can flower in as little as six weeks from planting without any special treatment. Just pot them up in the same way as for hyacinths and leave them in a cool, light spot to develop further.

Simplest of all, though, are varieties such as 'Paperwhite' and 'Cragford', which will grow happily just in water. A wide glass bowl or jar looks best, and this can be filled with gravel or even small pebbles. Lodge the bulbs in firmly to three-quarters of their depth, then fill up with water to just below the base of the bulbs.

planting can be a bit of a chore, but hang in there. You can use a trowel to make individual holes, but in soft ground, or after rain, a special bulb planter (which lifts out a plug of soil to the required depth) will be a help. Alternatively you can dig out the whole area, setting the bulbs in at twice their own width apart.

If your soil is heavy or liable to become soggy, add a 1/2 in/13mm layer of coarse sand to the planting hole. This helps drainage and prevents bulbs from rotting.

Once the bulbs are in, fill in with soil, then mark the spot with a short stake or large label. You may think you'll remember where you have planted everything, but you won't.

CONTAINER PLANTING

Planting in containers is much simpler. First make sure that your pot or tub has drainage holes. Then add a layer of gravel or broken crocks to cover the base and prevent the drainage holes from clogging up.

Free-draining potting mix is best for spring bulbs in outdoor containers, while a more moisture-retentive peat/perlite mix is fine for summer bulbs like lilies. In large tubs, which would be expensive to refill each year, you can compromise by replacing just the top few inches with fresh soil mix.

Set in the bulbs at the recommended depth, spacing them one bulb's-width apart, then fill in with more soil to within 1 in/2.5 cm of the rim and water in. Keep containers watered in warm, dry weather, but not in winter.

AFTERCARE

Protect against slugs by surrounding the plant with a barrier of sharp gravel or broken egg shells. Squirrels

can also become a problem, digging up and eating newly planted bulbs. If so, cover with wire mesh pinned in place with short sticks; remove the mesh once growth appears. To keep deer away, you may have to build a fence.

Remove faded flowers – if they are allowed to set seed, the bulb will be weakened, and whatever the bulb, leave it to die down naturally after flowering. The energy from the leaves is reabsorbed to form next year's flowers. Fertilize with a high-phosphorus food, such as bonemeal, after flowering to give them a boost.

Over several years, flowering may diminish because the bulbs have increased in number and become overcrowded. Dig them up carefully after flowering, separate them out and replant.

A mix and match planting of dwarf narcissus, crocuses, and netted irises.

HARMONIOUS PLANTING

Cheerful bulb mixes might seem tempting when planning a spring display, but you'll find that when viewed from a distance your riot of color has turned into a formless glob. Bulbs really do look their best and most natural when planted in single color groups.

That doesn't mean that they can't be teamed up with other bulbs and flowers, but keep it simple. Scillas and

primroses, for instance, relish the same conditions, and the soft blues and yellows harmonize beautifully. Or you could use the secret weapon of all spring gardeners – the forget-me-not. The sky-blue flowers, produced right through spring, are the perfect accompaniment for late daffodils and tulips. When flowering is over, they're simplicity itself to uproot and discard, leaving a scattering of

seedlings for next year's display.

And when you're planting, don't forget the natural backdrop against which your bulbs will flower. The purple globes of alliums, for instance, look wonderful with pink or white roses, creamy tulips are stunning against a dark green hedge, and white daffodils look quite magical when planted under striking white-bark birches.

Top Ten Bulbs

◆ ALLIUM
(Ornamental onion)
Brilliant bulbs for early summer, coinciding with the first flush of roses. Showy members of the humble onion family, two favorite species are *Allium christophii,* with its huge heads of metallic purple stars, and the incredible *Allium giganteum,* whose purple drumstick flowers can tower to 6 ft/1.8m. Easy to grow in a sunny, well-drained spot.

◆ *ANEMONE BLANDA*
A delight of early spring, low growing and needing no special care. The starry flowers of blue, pink, or white open when the sun

Anemone blanda

English bluebells

PLANTING TIPS

Make the most of space. If there is a large blank area under your deciduous shrubs in spring – fill it with bulbs. Once they have flowered, the shrub will be in leaf and obligingly hide their dying foliage.

To extend the flowering time, inter- plant late-blooming Darwin tulips with early-flowering Greigii type tulips. Their striped foliage remains attractive long after bloom time.

Taller varieties of daffodils and tulips are easily damaged by wind, so use the sturdier short-stemmed varieties in exposed locations.

The grape hyacinth, Muscari armeni- acum, is a pretty little thing, but it's a weed at heart and will self-seed all over the garden. Curb its enthusiasm by planting it in pots only.

shines, so it would be unwise to plant them in a shaded spot. Use them in beds, borders, or even in the lawn, where they will naturalize easily.

◆ SPANISH SQUILL AND ENGLISH BLUEBELL
These lovely blue flowers increase readily and are appropriate in informal parts of the garden, where they can spread freely. They prefer a moist soil, but in fact will grow almost anywhere, in sun or shade. Buy the bulbs early and plant immediately. Spanish squills are also available in pink and white.

◆ CROCUS
One of the earliest bright flowers of the year, with dainty semiwild varieties in early spring, followed by the larger hybrids in midspring. They can be planted in any sunny, well-drained spot but look their absolute best when they are naturalized in the lawn. Sparrows have an unexplained passion for tearing yellow ones to pieces.

◆ DAFFODIL (*Narcissus*)
The most welcome of spring flowers, giving the first really bold splash of color of the year, from as early as February. The range is enormous, with varieties suitable for window boxes, pots, beds, borders, and even for naturalizing in grass and under trees. Larger varieties like white 'Ice Follies' are commonly called daffodils, while "narcissus" is generally applied to wild species and smaller hybrids such as 'Téte-â-Téte' and 'February Gold'. Avoided by deer.

◆ HYACINTH
Because of their delicious perfume, hyacinths are great favorites for growing indoors, but they can also be used to give strong blocks of color in the garden in midspring, interplanted with daffodils or tulips. After the first year's flowering, the blossoms gradually become looser and can be transplanted for naturalizing elsewhere in the garden.

◆ IRIS

The early flowering hybrid netted irises are little gems. They appear in early spring, and although they're only 6 in/15cm tall, make a real impact. The sky blue 'Joyce' is one of the loveliest, and 'JS Dijt' is the best for scent. Be wary of yellow *Iris danfordiae,* which flowers for only one season. Give irises a sunny position, in light, free-draining soil.

◆ LILY

Of all the summer bulbs, this is the undoubted queen. And despite their exotic looks and fragrance, they're not difficult to grow – the only chore is staking the taller varieties. In the garden, they must have rich, well-drained soil, but they're perfect for pots, where with good soil and protection from slugs and deer they'll be magnificent. Start with a beauty like the white *Lilium regale* and you'll be hooked. But do look out for the cherry red lily beetle, which is becoming increasingly common – it devastates plants and there's no easy chemical control, so squash it on sight.

Snowdrops (Galanthus nivalis)

◆ SNOWDROP (*Galanthus nivalis*)

These delicate white flowers are a delight in the dark days of winter. They prefer a heavy, moist soil in partial shade, but in fact will grow in all but the driest locations. If clumps become too crowded, lift them immediately after flowering, tease out the smaller groups of bulbs, and replant them.

Lilies make spectacular and long-lasting cut flowers.

◆ TULIP

In color, and in form, this is the most astonishingly varied of all spring bulbs, and if you pick your varieties well you'll have a succession of flower for a full three months. Early varieties include low growers such as *T. kaufmanniana* 'Scarlet Baby', which are perfect for window boxes, while the season ends in late spring with an explosion of color from taller types like 'Estelle Rijnveld', one of the outrageously frilled and feathered parrot-type tulips. But if you want to establish tulips permanently, remember their two essential requirements: a deep, free-draining soil and a sunny south-facing location, where they can enjoy a good baking.

Climbers and wall shrubs

Climbing plants are invaluable for giving the garden a well-furnished, finished look. And as a bonus, if you have anything to hide (an ugly wall, a dilapidated shed), they'll do it beautifully.

W e'll be introducing you to some of the better wall shrubs here, too – plants like ceanothus and

Clematis flowers

pyracantha, which will benefit from the warmth and shelter of a wall, and add height and interest. So although they're not climbers, they deserve honorary membership.

GROWING SUCCESS

Climbers are long-lived plants, with a lot of growing to do, so it pays to give them a good start. First, of course, you must choose a healthy plant. Sturdy stems are a good sign but most important of all are the roots. Tip the pot and check the drainage holes – reject any with a mass of roots, but those with just a few roots emerging are at exactly the right stage for planting.

Preparing the planting site is dull work, but vital for success, so don't take short cuts, especially when you're planting close to walls where the soil is usually poor and dry. It's doubly important when planting a climber to grow up a tree, where it will always face fierce competition from the tree's roots.

First water the plant thoroughly, then dig a hole that's twice the width of the container and 12 in/30cm deep. Ideally, set the hole at least 18 in/45cm from the wall or tree, though in confined spaces this isn't always possible. Improve the excavated soil by mixing it with equal parts organic matter, such as compost or well-rotted manure.

Now carefully tip the plant out of the pot and free any roots that have wound around the rootball. Place the plant in the hole, checking that the surface of the soil is

at ground level, and spread out the loosened roots. Fill in with your soil mix, firming gently as you go and being careful not to leave air pockets. If the stems are not yet long enough to reach the wall, tie them on to angled bamboo stakes so that they're heading in the right direction. Water well and keep evenly moist for the next few months.

SUPPORTING

Some climbers, such as ivy and *Hydrangea petiolaris*, are self-supporting, attaching themselves by little aerial roots, and need no help to scale a wall. Most Virginia creepers have special sucker pads on their tendrils. But the twiners (honeysuckle, clematis, wisteria, and the like) must have something to hang on to.

A framework of garden wire stretched between vine eyes (masonry nails with a hole at the end) is your cheapest option. But take note: the

Planting *Holes for climbers should be at least 18 in/45cm from walls and 8 in/20cm from pillars and free-standing trellises. Insert stakes to act as guides for new shoots.*

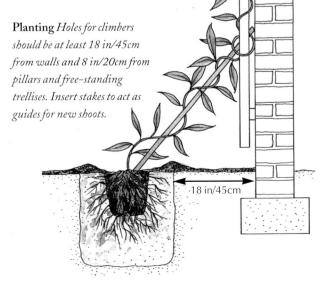

-18 in/45cm

Making the most of Clematis

Clematis is a treasure among climbers, with its glorious blooms, wonderful range of colors, and long flowering period.

The large-flowered hybrids are the most immediately attractive and make a splendid show, most of them growing to no more than a neat 10 ft/3m. But small-flowered types have their virtues, too. *Clematis montana* makes a dense cover for unsightly walls and buildings and will clamber up through large trees with reckless abandon, filling them with a mass of blossom in late spring. *Clematis alpina* is much less vigorous (6 ft/1.8m) but supremely delicate, with finely cut leaves and nodding spring flowers.

There are just two mysteries attached to clematis. The first is pruning, and we hope that our guidelines will help you there. The second is the dreaded clematis wilt, which plant scientists have had great difficulty explaining. It's a dramatic

Clematis *'Perle d'Azur'*

disease – the plant collapses and dies virtually overnight. Young plants are most susceptible, but a little extra attention will help prevent it.

Most important of all is to plant deeply – 4 in/10cm deeper than the plant was in the pot – so that if anything happens to the top growth, there will be dormant buds underground ready to take over. And try to choose a location where the roots are shaded from the sun. If this is not possible, cover the roots well with mulch to keep them cool. Then in the first year of growth, keep the plant lavishly watered and give it a monthly feeding with any general-purpose liquid fertilizer during the summer. If, despite all your efforts, wilt does strike, cut back all the top growth and wait – it's quite likely that new growth will spring from the base.

CLEMATIS PRUNING
Clematis differ in their pruning needs, and while it would be impossible to mention every single

cultivar, this is a summary of those you're most likely to find at the garden center or nursery.

No pruning: These smaller-flowered species clematis need no pruning at all, but you can cut them back after flowering if they have outgrown their allotted space: *C. alpina, armandii, cirrhosa, macropetala, montana, orientalis, tangutica.*

Light pruning: Large-flowered hybrids, flowering in late spring/early summer and often again in fall, need only light pruning in early spring, just to keep the plant tidy. *C.* 'Barbara Jackman', 'Bees' Jubilee', 'Doctor Ruppel', 'Duchess of Edinburgh', 'Elsa Spaeth', *florida* 'Sieboldii', 'Henryi', 'Lady Northcliffe', 'Lasurstern', 'Lincoln Star', 'Marie Boisselot', 'Miss Bateman', 'Mrs. Cholmondeley', 'Nelly Moser', 'Richard Pennell', 'The President', 'Vyvyan Pennell'.

Hard pruning: Summer-flowering clematis, for the most part, should be cut back hard in late winter, taking all stems to within 18 in/50cm of the ground – it sounds drastic, but is essential. *C.* 'Comtesse de Bouchaud', 'Ernest Markham', 'Gipsy Queen', 'Hagley Hybrid', × *jackmanii* (all), 'Lady Betty Balfour', 'Madame Baron Veillard', 'Madame Edouard Andre', 'Niobe', 'Perle d'Azur', 'Rouge Cardinal', 'Ville de Lyon', *viticella* (any).

Clematis *'Nelly Moser'*

wire will sag under a heavy plant if not really taut, and it's going to be very difficult to get to the wall if you want to paint or repair it.

Plastic netting is a good choice for the less vigorous climbers and can be stretched between hooks so that both mesh and plant can be detached and lowered to the ground if you need access to the wall. Bulkier climbers would be safer with a sheet of rigid plastic mesh.

A wooden trellis is the most expensive option, but very decorative. Attaching it top and bottom to horizontal battens, and using hinges at the bottom and hooks and eyes at the top, allows the whole contraption to be moved away from the wall, if need be. This has the added advantage that the trellis is not flat against the wall, and plants can twine in and out freely.

TYING IN

Whether your plant is a clinger or a twiner, it will need a little training to make a good, even cover. Tie in new growths with plastic-covered plant ties rather than string (which rots) or wire (which can damage soft stems). Twist the ties so that they're secure, but never knot them – as the stems thicken, a knotted tie can bite in and strangle them, whereas a twisted tie will give.

AFTERCARE

Watering: Climbers on walls or near trees need extra water in warm, dry weather, even when they're well established. Give them a thorough watering with a hose,

NORTH WALLS

A sunless wall might seem an inhospitable place for climbers and wall shrubs, but as long as it isn't overshadowed by nearby buildings, a surprising number of plants will thrive there.

The all-purpose ivy, in any of the plain green or the variegated forms with white or gold markings on the leaves, will be perfectly happy, as will that other adaptable plant, *Euonymus fortunei* 'Silver Queen', a variegated shrub that, remarkably, turns into a climber if you position it against a wall.

Pyracanthas, too. We tend to associate them with sunny spots, but as long as they're not in constant wind, they'll enjoy the shelter of the wall and produce a good crop of berries. Winter jasmine *(Jasminum nudiflorum)*, with its wands of gold flowers through winter, is another showy plant that does well.

For large expanses of wall, any of the Virginia creepers *(Parthenocissus)* will do well, providing good cover and wonderful fall color. And *Hydrangea petiolaris* and *Schizophragma integrifolium* are two other vigorous climbers to treasure for a north wall, with their lacy white flowerheads. Schizophragma isn't easy to find, but well worth tracking down.

And how about clematis? Any number of them flower well in a north-facing position, but just to get you going, take your pick from white 'Marie Boisselot', shell-pink 'Hagley Hybrid', mauve-pink 'Nelly Moser', violet 'Vyvyan Pennell' (one of the best of the double-flowered clematis), sky blue 'Perle d'Azur', and deep purple *jackmanii* and 'The President'.

rather than a shower from the garden sprinkler.
Feeding: A spring feeding of rose fertilizer gives all climbers and wall shrubs an annual boost. At the same time, mulch with a layer of well-rotted manure or compost to improve the soil, lock in moisture, and keep the weeds down.
Pruning: To keep plants within bounds, and to create a good shape, some pruning is inevitable. Light pruning can be done at any time during the growing season, to any climber or wall shrub (though obviously it would be wiser not to do it when they're in bud or flower), but the rules for more severe pruning differ from plant to plant. To make it easier for you, you'll find pruning times and methods alongside the main plants featured here.

Top Ten Climbers and Wall Shrubs

• CEANOTHUS Zones 7-10

A mature ceanothus, covered in a mist of blue flowers, is breathtaking. An ideal wall shrub for sun, as long as you have room to accommodate its spreading habit. Of the evergreen hybrids, look out for bright blue 'Burkwoodii' (10 ft/3m), soft blue 'Autumnal Blue' (10 ft/3m) and powder-blue 'Cascade' (12 ft/3.6m) – this last has a lovely arching habit. Evergreen ceanothus should never be pruned hard – you risk killing it. Instead, just lightly trim back the side shoots after flowering.

GROWING TIPS

People worry about climbers damaging their walls, but there's no need. If the wall is sound to start with, the climber will in fact protect it from the weather and keep it in better condition than an unplanted wall.

Be very cautious about planting a silver-lace vine (Polygonum aubertii). It grows rapidly and will take over your garden, your house, and you, if you stand still long enough.

For a sunny fence or wall, don't forget the annual climbers. Sweet peas are a must (see our section on growing from seed), and other delights include orange black-eyed Susan vine (Thunbergia alata), sky blue morning glory (Ipomoea), and orange-red Chilean glory flower (Eccremocarpus scaber).

• CLEMATIS ZONES 4-7

The essential climber. The large-flowered hybrids and rampant *montana* varieties are justifiably popular, but you might like to investigate some of the more unusual members of this remarkable family. The evergreen *C. armandii* 'Apple Blossom' is lovely for a sheltered spot – with large strap-shaped leaves and pale pink, scented flowers in early spring. *C. tangutica* and *C. orientalis* have ferny leaves and small bell-shaped blooms in bright yellow, produced from late summer through fall.

• *HEDERA* (Ivy) Zones 4-9

One of the most adaptable of all climbers, with a terrific variety of leaf form and color. The golden forms are great for a sunny spot – the green/gold leaves of *H. hibernica* 'Sulphurea', for instance, or the daintier 'Buttercup', which is entirely gold in full sun. A good tip on speed of growth is that, in general, large-leaved forms are more vigorous than small-leaved,

Jasminum nudiflorum

Hydrangea petiolaris

and that plain green varieties put on more of a sprint than the variegated ones. Ivies can be pruned as hard as you like in spring.

• *HYDRANGEA PETIOLARIS* (Climbing hydrangea) Zones 4-8

Slow to establish, but once it gets going, this self-clinging climber can soar to 50 ft/15m, covered in large white lacecap flowers in early summer. If this is too tall, you might like to try one of its close relatives, *Schizophragma integrifolium*, which will reach a mere 30 ft/9m. The midsummer flowers are interesting – an inner circle of tiny florets, surrounded by dangling white bracts. Neither plant needs regular pruning, but can be cut back after flowering.

• *JASMINUM NUDIFLORUM* (Winter jasmine) Zones 5-10

With its bright yellow flowers from early winter to spring, this is an invaluable shrub (to 10 ft/3m) for a north-facing location, but will also thrive in a sunny spot. The long, whippy stems should be tied in to a support and allowed to cascade forward. Prune after flowering, thinning out a few of the older stems to encourage new growth.

◆ *LONICERA PERICLYMENUM* (Honeysuckle) Zones 4-8

Valued for their incomparable scent, honeysuckles like an airy position in sun or part shade. They twine and need support on a wall, but will happily scramble unaided up trees. Two of the showiest are the late spring-flowering 'Belgica', and 'Serotina', which flowers summer through fall. Both grow to 15 ft/4.5m or more. The rampant semievergreen *L. japonica* 'Halliana' has simpler creamy white blooms, but flowers non-stop from mid-summer to late autumn. Prune after flowering and thin out some of the older stems. If plants become hopelessly tangled and scrawny-looking, cut right back to the main stems in early spring.

◆ *PARTHENOCISSUS* Zones 3-9

All the plants in this group, including Virginia creeper, are excellent for covering a vast expanse, very quickly. They're self-clinging and have the charming habit, when no wall space remains, of hanging down in great festoons. The fall color is spectacular. *P. tricuspidata* 'Veitchii' (Boston ivy) is one of the best, for its glossy apple-green leaves and neat uniform growth to 50 ft/15m. No pruning needed, but can be cut back in spring if necessary.

◆ *PYRACANTHA* (Firethorn) Zones 6-9

An excellent wall shrub for sun, with glossy evergreen leaves and small white flowers followed by red, orange, or gold berries. 'Orange Glow' is especially good. To keep them flat to the wall, they need to be firmly attached. The long shoots can be cut back after flowering (wear gloves – the thorns are vicious) to

Solanum crispum *'Glasnevin'*

Pyracantha

keep the plant compact. They grow to around 10 ft/3m, with a similar spread, but can be cut to shape to make a formal feature (around a door, for instance), though this inevitably limits flowering and berrying.

◆ *SOLANUM CRISPUM* 'GLASNEVIN' (Chilean potato tree) Zones 8-10

A scrambling wall shrub for a sunny spot, with large heads of blue-purple flowers right through summer. 20 ft/6m. Easy to please, but rather lax growth, so looks better when trained against a wall. Prune in spring, taking out old or damaged growths and shortening any stragglers. The white *S. jasminoides* 'Alba' is very similar but not quite so hardy.

◆ WISTERIA Zones 4-9

The classic climber, with a spectacular early summer waterfall of flowers, but must have a south or west wall. Try to buy grafted plants – cheaper seed-raised plants can take up to 12 years to flower. And check the eventual height before you buy; *W. sinensis* can reach 100 ft/30m, while *W. floribunda* grows to a much

more manageable 30 ft/9m. A solid, woody plant, wisteria needs very firm wall support, and a pruning regime is essential for good flowering. In summer, cut back all side shoots (there will be plenty) to around 6 in/15cm, leaving six buds. In winter, reduce these same shoots by a further 2 in/5cm or so, so that only two or three buds remain.

IDEAS FOR LOW-MAINTENANCE

That most versatile of all climbers, ivy, can be used to make remarkably handsome ground cover. It forms a dense, weed-suppressing carpet and looks especially good under trees.

When buying climbers, pay close attention to the label, noting the eventual height. A vigorous climber in a restricted space will need regular and time-consuming pruning.

The ground close to walls is usually exceedingly dry, and plants will need extra water in summer. To minimize this chore, spread an organic mulch around the base of the plant – this looks attractive, keeps the roots cooler, and reduces loss of water by evaporation.

Vary the look of your garden by surrounding permanent plants with cheerful summer annuals.

Container gardening

Virtually anything can be grown in containers, from colorful annuals and tasty vegetables to scented climbers, even small trees. And virtually anything can be used as a container, from old shoes and paint cans to the more traditional terracotta pots and wooden barrels.

When you plant in containers, you're making the most of all available space – brightening up a gloomy corner, cheering up a plantless patio. You can even shuffle the pots around for an instant change of scene.

GROWING SUCCESS

Container plants do need a little more care than those in the open ground, but this form of 'gardening in miniature' gives you numerous opportunities for change and for some really exquisite effects.

SOIL

It really is important to use good soil. Resist the temptation to save money by using garden soil; it's not the right consistency for container gardening, and it can harbor pests and diseases, so your plants will inevitably have to struggle.

For shrubs, climbers, or trees, which are likely to remain in the same container for several years, use a soil-based potting mix. Herbs and bulbs, too, will appreciate the excellent drainage that this type of mix provides.

Peat-based mixes are ideal for bedding plants, vegetables, or anything that's being planted for just a few months. They are generally called "soilless" potting mix and contain perlite or vermiculite as well as peat moss. It is lighter in weight than soil-based mixes.

Ericaceous mixes are specially formulated for acid-loving plants such as rhododendrons, azaleas, camellias, and Japanese andromedas.

DRAINAGE

Whatever container you're using, it's essential that it's well drained to prevent waterlogging. So check that it has drainage holes – most do, but some, like wooden barrels, have solid bases. If this is the case, you'll have to drill holes (five well-spaced $1/2$ in/13mm holes would be ideal in this instance).

The other golden rule is to add drainage material to the base of the container. This prevents soil from being washed away when you water and from blocking up the drainage holes. Broken clay pots (shards) or small

With their dazzling colors and pretty "faces", pansies are superb container plants.

PLANTING FOR A SHADY SITE

Unless it's permanently dark, any shady paved area that catches just a little sun can become home to a remarkable variety of plants in pots. Many summer bedding plants, such as fuchsias and impatiens, will flourish, but it's the foliage plants that really beautify a shady spot.

Ferns are naturals for this sort of situation. All too often they look wispy and uninviting at the garden center, but they can grow into magnificent plants. Evergreen species with light green fronds are perfect, one of the best being the soft shield fern, *Polystichum setiferum* and its

cultivars. Hostas will love it too, so exploit all their colors, from blue-gray to white-variegated, and their sculptural leaf shapes.

Dead nettles, which are vigorous spreaders, can be tamed in pots and are ideal for shade, especially the white- or silver-variegated forms, though it would be best to shear them now and again to keep them compact. Another rampant plant is baby's tears, which is usually sold as a houseplant, although it is hardy in zones 9 and 10. It makes a beautiful green cushion of tiny leaves in a pot – but never let it anywhere near a patch of open ground.

Japanese andromeda will give you a cascade of evergreen foliage with the bonus of spring flowers and flaming red young shoots, and Japanese maples will provide the icing on the cake. Expensive and slow-growing, they're exquisite small trees for pots. The cut-leaved varieties, whether plain green or reddish-purple, are the most delightful of all.

Using the plants mentioned here will result in a subtle container garden. If you want to jazz it up, add some camellias, azaleas, rhododendrons, hydrangeas, and a few gold-variegated shrubs, depending on your zone.

stones are ideal for smaller containers, and broken bricks can be used in larger ones. Don't skimp on it; use a 1-2 in/2.5-5cm layer in medium to large pots and up to 6 in/15cm in the very largest barrels.

PLANTING

After adding the drainage material, fill in with soil mix to within 1 in/2.5cm or so of the rim of the container, firming it down but not squashing it. Using a hand trowel, dig individual holes for each of the plants, taking care that they're set in at the same level as they were in the original pot. Gently firm the soil around them, adding more if needed. Water thoroughly until you see the excess running out of the bottom of the container.

WATERING

From then on, the amount of watering required depends on the time of year and location of the container (if it's in a sunny spot, it will need more watering than one in shade). You'll also find that larger containers dry out less quickly than smaller ones, and that plastic pots need less water than clay.

The most difficult thing is to tell whether to water or not. The simple answer is to check each container regularly in the summer – put your finger into the soil mix, and if it feels dry more than 1 in/2.5cm beneath the surface, then it needs watering. In sunny locations, smaller pots may need daily or even twice daily watering, and larger ones three times a week or more.

Trailing or low-growing plants such as this viola can be used to soften the edges of your container planting.

For the rest of the year, it's much simpler – a weekly check should be sufficient. By the way, don't assume that your pots will have been well watered if it's been raining. Dense foliage can deflect the rain, and even after a heavy shower the soil could still be dry.

FEEDING

Four or five weeks after planting, the fertilizer in the soil mix will be running out. Seasonal plants – fruit, vegetables, and summer annuals – are greedy and will need routine weekly feedings of high-potassium fertilizer such as liquid tomato food. Permanent plants need only two applications of a general all-purpose fertilizer – one in spring and the second in early summer. Feeding is important for the health of the plants; in the garden the roots can go exploring for food, but in a container the plants must rely on you to maintain the soil fertility.

REPOTTING

A vigorous plant such as a tree or a shrub will occasionally need to be repotted into a larger container and usually shows it by growing much less vigorously. Water such a plant well, wait an hour, then remove it from the pot and place it in the new container, filling in with fresh soil mix.

TOPPING UP

When plants reach maturity and are permanently settled, it's a good idea to freshen the soil mix each year by removing the top 2-4 in/5-10cm in spring and adding a layer of new soil mix.

CREATING A TOPIARY
Boxwood *(Buxus)* is one of the easiest of all shrubs to train into a decorative shape. Pinch out the growing tips of the young plant to encourage bushiness (1), then trim regularly but lightly to shape (2). Transplant to larger pots as needed – once mature, it will need only an occasional haircut with the shears (3).

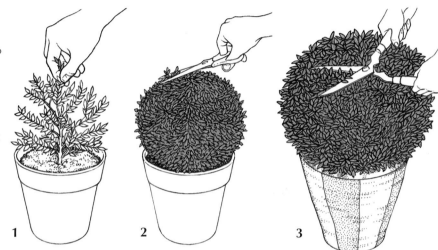

1   2   3

DECORATIVE CLAY CONTAINERS

Clay pots are our number one favorites when it comes to containers. The sturdy simplicity of the plain clay pot is always pleasing, but there are some wonderfully decorative pots available from garden centers and specialty catalogs.

Some decorative pots have a crimped edge, and the smaller ones look especially pretty when planted with simple flowers like primroses, which echo the pot's wavy rim. Other pots are decorated with twisted ribbons of clay. Pots can also be beautifully shaped – some are delightfully squat and fat-bellied, while others are long and elegant.

The fanciest (and most expensive) of all are the Italian-style pots, adorned with a riot of swags and garlands, which look most effective if you use them for just one striking plant. Or put in two or three plants of one color and variety; an Italian pot planted with pink ivy-leaved geraniums will be a show-stopper all summer.

Some pots are so handsome that they can be left empty. Curvy "Ali Baba" jars, wide-shouldered Greek oil jars, and all types of outsized urns can look wonderful set in the border or used as a focal point for a favorite planting.

Clay looks better the older it gets, and antique pots command premium prices because of the patina of age they have acquired. But a brand new pot can be 'aged' within months rather than years if you brush it with diluted fertilizer or yogurt – it'll soon take on that soft, weathered look.

Making the most of your Container

As we said previously, virtually anything that holds soil can be used as a plant container but when you've run through your supply of old shoes, paint cans, and mop buckets, it could be time for a trip to the garden center to stock up with something more conventional.

Clay pots, plain or fancy, are the most desirable of all containers. They're heavy and stable and their natural warm color complements all plants, particularly as the clay mellows with age. The downside is that they ARE heavy, and awkward to move around when you want to rearrange your display. They are often expensive, especially the antique ones and those made and decorated by hand. Not only are the breakable, but they must be brought indoors in cold winter climates to avoid the cracking and chipping induced by the very cold temperatures. Terra cotta is porous, allowing oxygen rich air to supply the plants roots, while allowing excess soil moisture to escape. Some gardeners feel that this protects them from watering errors, but means that the pots require more frequent watering during the hot days of summer. In spite of the disadvantages, their ability to blend into the garden far outweighs them.

OTHER MATERIALS

Containers made of fiberglass are gaining in popularity, especially in large sizes, in spite of their relatively high cost. They are lightweight and durable, and can be left out of doors through the worst weather. They are made plain or fancy with a finish to

simulate lead, bronze, cast iron, slate or other elegant, traditional materials. Because of their light weight they are especially useful for terrace or balcony plantings where weight is an important consideration.

Plastic containers are inexpensive and long lasting. Available in many colors to suit most situations, they withstand frost and are easy to clean. They too are light in weight. Unfortunately the less expensive ones may become brittle in strong sun, and need to be replaced after only one or two seasons. Synthetic materials are also used to make imitation clay pots, and some are pretty convincing.

Wooden tubs, planter boxes and half-barrels are good value but should be treated with a non-toxic wood preservation such as Cuprinol to prevent rotting. Although higher

Petunias, daisies, and helichrysum bask in a fluted clay pot, backed by pink nicotianas.

priced than others, those constructed from cedar or black locust are more durable and require no wood preservatives. As an additional precaution against decay, it helps if you line the inside with plastic; be sure to make plenty of drainage holes in the bottom so that water can drain away readily. Ready made wooden boxes usually come with a rigid liner insert. It is wise to support tubs and barrels on bricks or specially designed "pot feet", so that the bottom of the barrel can drain freely and avoid rotting.

Glazed pots are becoming increasingly popular, partly because they tend to be cheaper than plain clay.

Top Plants for Container Gardening

❖ BEDDING PLANTS

Top performers for summer include marguerites, dwarf nicotiana, verbena, geraniums, and fuchsias. For contrast, add attractive foliage plants like silver-leaved dusty miller and helichrysum or ferny-leaved Swan River daisy (*Brachycome*). Later color can be provided by chrysanthemums, which come in varied colors and last well into early winter. And primroses look especially good in smaller pots early in the year. The keys to success with all these plants are constant removal of spent flowers and, in summer, regular watering and feeding.

❖ BULBS

You can create a terrific long-lasting spring display by planting a number of pots, each with a different variety: for example, species *Crocus* 'Snowbunting' which flowers in early spring; dwarf *Narcissus* 'Quail' to follow; and still later, one of the best tulip varieties, the dwarf, 'Red Riding Hood'. For summer color, grow blue or white African lilies, which thrive in sunny spots. And lilies are magnificent and easy to grow (for a real show, plant three bulbs in a 10 in/25cm pot).

A spring planting of daffodils, tulips, hyacinths, and muscari fill a box.

◆ CLIMBERS

All but the most vigorous climbers will grow in containers. Large-flowered clematis are excellent, as are honeysuckles, summer and winter jasmine, and the colorful variegated ivies. Annual climbers such as black-eyed Susan vine (*Thunbergia*) and morning glory (*Ipomoea*) are fast-growing and eye-catching choices for pots in sunny spots. For perennial climbers, choose a pot big enough for at least two years' growth – if you find this hard to estimate, check with a plant expert at your garden center.

◆ FRUIT

It often surprises people that fruit can be grown in pots. Top fruit (tree fruit such as apples) needs large pots, up to half- barrel size. Be sure to buy varieties on dwarfed stock. Few of the bush fruits are happy in containers, though red, white, and black currants do well. Without doubt, the most successful of all are strawberries, which not only look good but give excellent crops. Plant either singly in 4 in/ 10cm pots or in special strawberry jars with side planting holes. All fruit needs to be grown in a sunny location.

◆ HERBS

Herbs grow well in containers and are particularly rewarding – they're troublefree, grow quickly, look good together, and smell wonderful. Some, like thyme, marjoram, and sage, are available in golden and variegated forms and can be used very effectively to contrast with other plants. Trained bay laurel looks magnificent in pots, but needs winter protection in colder areas. Most herbs do best in sunny spots and can put up with a bit of drought (when you forget to water them). Mint is the main exception, needing to be kept moist, so place a saucer under the pot and keep it filled with water in summer.

Clematis can be trained to climb up a decorative trellis.

These herbs are growing in a special strawberry jar, with holes in the sides.

◆ ROSES

Many modern roses have been bred for compact, bushy growth and almost continuous flower, making them ideal for pots. Patio roses, in particular, are superb. They are larger and more robust versions of miniature roses, with charming flowers and a neat growth habit. A popular one is bright scarlet 'Starina' (12 in/30cm). Climbing roses can be extremely vigorous, so search out shorter varieties like the 8 ft/2.4m 'Golden Showers'. To thrive, container-grown roses need a reasonably sunny spot and a feeding with rose fertilizer twice a year, in spring and early summer. The one disadvantage is that they can look dull in winter, so tuck in a few small foliage plants, such as variegated ivies, to brighten them up.

◆ SHRUBS

Some of the most useful shrubs are those that look good year-round. Flowering evergreens like camellias, rhododendrons, Mexican orange, and winter-flowering *Viburnum tinus* 'Compactum' are good choices. Some evergreens are

Rhododendron yakushimanum

grown purely for their attractive foliage: huge-leaved *Fatsia japonica*, spiky phormiums and cordylines, and many conifers are worth considering. In shadier spots, try any of the gold-spotted aucuba or *Euonymus fortunei* 'Emerald 'n' Gold', one of the finest gold-variegated dwarf evergreens. Make your selection according to your hardiness zone (see Zone Map page 156-7).

✦ TREES

Nothing else provides such a dramatic instant effect as a tree does, and any of the smaller trees can be grown very successfully in larger tubs. Cut-leaved Japanese maples (*Acer palmatum* cultivars) are particularly good for shade, while weeping *Cotoneaster salicifolius* 'Pendulus' is good in sun. As for flowering trees, crab apples (*Malus*) must come to the top of the list – 'Red Jade' is one of the

very best, with white spring blossom followed by abundant red fruits. Be bold – any tree that attracts your eye and grows to around 12 ft/ 3.6m will be perfectly happy in a large tub or half-barrel.

✦ VEGETABLES

Vegetables in containers can look surprisingly decorative – zucchini, for instance, have beautiful leaves. The most rewarding are those that yield the biggest crop from the smallest area – climbing plants like pole beans and snap peas and fast-maturing plants like lettuce and radishes. Tomatoes are great, especially the tasty cherry-sized 'Sweet 100' and 'Yellow Canary', with bumper crops even in a 10 in/25cm pot. Peppers are very ornamental, especially the varieties that bear colorful fruits.

Peppers are easy to grow in containers.

IDEAS FOR LOW-MAINTENANCE

Watering is probably the most time-consuming chore, and the following tips will help minimize it.

- *Line the inside of large clay pots with plastic before planting, remembering to make drainage holes at the bottom.*
- *Give pots a thorough soaking – a surface dribble from a hose or watering can won't last long at all.*
- *Water-retaining crystals (which swell up into a gel when mixed with water) can be added to the soil before planting. Acting as a reservoir they reduce the frequency of watering by half.*
- *A 1 in/2.5cm layer of gravel on the surface of the pot keeps roots cooler in sunny spots and helps prevent loss of moisture by evaporation.*
- *The bigger the container, the less frequently it will need watering, so it may pay to think big when planting.*

Rather than feeding your plants with liquid fertilizer on a regular basis in summer, incorporate some slow-release fertilizer granules in the soil mix when planting. These will feed the plants for you very effectively all season (and save the bother of trying to remember when your plants were last fed).

Instead of planting lots of new containers with seasonal plants every few months, use good permanent potted plants in the background and concentrate on changing seasonal displays in a few pots clustered in front of them.

Permanent plants and herbs need far less attention than annuals and vegetables, which are colorful and fun, but quite time consuming. Consider using a selection of herbs with variegated foliage for added interest.

Fruit

A succulent, sun-warmed strawberry; a sweet, ripe pear dripping juice down your chin; a crisp, rosy apple fresh from the tree – all it takes to grow fruit is a finely tuned set of taste buds, and a little care.

Ripening plums.

F ruit trees and bushes can be beautiful in their own right – apple blossoms in spring, fruit-laden trees in autumn, the gleam of golden raspberries and the translucent globes of gooseberries. A feast for the eye as well as the stomach. The fruits we recommend here are all on our "easy" list – those that you can grow with a minimum of fuss to produce maximum crops. Have a try. It's tremendously satisfying.

GROWING SUCCESS

Most fruit needs a sunny location, though raspberries, currants, and gooseberries will tolerate some shade.

Bearing fruit year after year is hard on plants, so give them the best possible start by enriching the soil with generous quantities of well-rotted manure or other organic material.

Place container-grown fruit at the same level in the ground as it was in the pot, and bare-root plants (available in the dormant season) with the junction of stem and roots just below soil level (there will be a dark soil mark to guide you), spreading the roots as wide as possible.

Water plants regularly during their first summer; in future years, tree fruits benefit greatly from a thorough watering during prolonged dry spells. Feed with a high-

Strawberries are one of the easiest fruits to grow successfully, even in the smallest garden. The heaviest crops are produced in the first few years, so replace your plants once fruiting starts to diminish with fresh specimens.

potassium fertilizer such as rose food in spring and add a mulch of organic matter like compost or well-rotted manure to keep the soil in good condition.

Pruning varies according to the type of fruit, and we have advocated the simplest possible methods for each one. One important tip – always cut just above an outward facing side shoot or bud.

If you grow and take care of your fruit, serious problems are unlikely. The most common are covered in the chapter on pests and diseases (see page 89), but if a problem is specific to a particular fruit, you'll find it described here.

CREATE A FEATURE

Mature apple and pear trees, with their dark, gnarled branches, have great dignity and presence in the garden and can easily be one of its most striking features.

Enhance them even further by using them as a support for a climbing plant such as a rose or clematis. But do a little homework first. Choose a climber that won't overwhelm the tree, but will ramble through it to a reasonable height. And when selecting clematis, opt for summer- rather than spring-flowering varieties. They'll take over when the tree's blossoms are just a happy memory.

Pear trees are easy to espalier against a wall.

WELL-TRAINED FRUIT

Sounds tricky? Not at all – training fruit trees, especially into cordons or espaliers, is a great way of saving space and not nearly so difficult as you might think.

Cordon apples and pears are grown on a single unbranched stem against a wall or fence. Buy a pre-trained tree and plant it at an angle of around 45°, secured to a bamboo stake – several trees set 3 ft/90cm apart look especially effective and you can mix and match varieties that cross-pollinate. Prune each in late summer, first cutting back any new shoots from the main stem to 3 in/7.5cm. Then turn your attention to the shoots that were pruned last year – they will have formed smaller sideshoots which should be pruned back to 1 in/2.5cm. And that's it! You've just trained a fruit tree.

Espaliers are a kind of living fence, with three or more matching pairs of branches trained horizontally from the main stem. Again, start with a pre-trained tree, tie it in to wires, and prune it in the same way as cordons. Espaliers can be grown against walls or fences or be installed as a fruitful divider between one part of the garden and another.

Once you get the bug for trained trees, you might want to try other forms, like fans, pyramids, and even low-growing mini-fences. If you do, seek guidance from the Brooklyn Botanic Garden handbook: *Growing Fruits*.

SELECTING FRUIT FOR THE SMALL GARDEN

In small gardens, fruit might seem like a luxury, but there are plenty of ways to tuck in a few plants so you can enjoy that fresh-picked flavor.

Strawberries grow well in pots and, even better, in hanging baskets, where they'll be safe from even the most athletic slug. Raspberries can be set along a fence and blackberries and loganberries trained against a wall.

Dwarf apples take up very little space – those on the dwarfest rootstocks do well in a large pot or half-barrel. Gooseberries and red currants will also thrive in pots or tubs, and you can have fun creating a gooseberry "tree" by training it on a single stem, taking out all the side shoots as they emerge, and leaving the top growth to bush out.

And don't overlook the ornamental value of tree fruits. Crab apples *(Malus)*, for instance, are beautiful small trees in their own right, with a wealth of spring blossoms, and masses of brightly colored fruits in fall that make a delicious jelly.

Apple and pear colonnades are an ideal choice for the small garden.

Essential Fruit Facts

Apple 'Sunset'

✦ APPLES

For good crops you need two compatible varieties that will cross-pollinate, and garden centers and fruit growers have charts to help you. One of the few exceptions is the new self-fertile Cox's Orange Pippin, which can be grown on its own.

Trees on dwarfing rootstocks are best for small gardens, and the approximate mature heights for these are:

M27	5 ft/1.5m
M9	8 ft/2.4m
M26	10 ft/3m
MM106	12 ft/3.6m

Apples need a warm, sheltered spot, planted at a distance apart that equals their mature height. The tiniest trees, on M27 and M9, need a rich soil to do well, and because the roots lack vigor, should be staked all their lives to keep them firmly anchored. Other rootstocks need only be staked (to 2 ft/60cm) for the first two or three years.

Pruning is largely a matter of common sense, and although there are special techniques to encourage extra fruiting, a well-shaped, healthy tree will naturally crop well. The aim is to create an open, goblet shape, so that all parts of the tree receive their fair share of air and sunshine.

In the first winter after planting, take out the leading stem, leaving three or four well-spaced side shoots, which should be cut back by two-thirds at this stage – they will eventually become the main branches. By the following winter, they will have thickened and produced their own side shoots. Cut back the long new growths of these branches by half and do the same to the side shoots (removing any that are rubbing or that cross the center of the tree).

Thereafter, remove any vigorous upright stems in summer and keep the tree trimmed to shape in winter, shortening long, whippy stems and removing crossing or weak growths. A few varieties bear fruit only at the tips of the branches, so if yours does this, prune out a third of the fruited shoots each winter, to encourage fresh growth.

Remove any fruits in the first summer, to build up a strong tree.

Troubleshooting

Brown rot, with concentric rings of white mold, is caused by a fungus entering damaged fruit. Remove and destroy affected apples.

Bitter pit causes brown flecking of skin and flesh and a bitter flavor. It is most prevalent after a hot, dry summer, so water deeply during any dry spells.

Scab appears as brown, woody patches and is worst in humid weather and on dense trees. Prune to keep the tree open and destroy any affected fruits and fallen leaves.

The caterpillars of the codling moth feed inside the apple and tunnel their way out when the fruit is ripe. Hang pheromone traps in the trees from late spring, to lure the male moths before mating begins.

Woolly aphids on stems and trunks cover themselves in a fluffy white "cotton". They do no great harm and can simply be washed off with the hose.

Recommended varieties

Eating: 'Jonagold', 'Braeburn', 'Gala', 'Golden Delicious', 'Granny Smith'.

Cooking: 'Jonared', 'Cortland'.

✦ BLACKBERRIES

Blackberries are long-lived, easy plants and can tolerate some shade. Support the rambling canes (stems) on a framework of four or five wires stretched between posts, to a height of around 6 ft/1.8m. One exception is the non-rambling 'Loch Ness', which can be grown in the same way as raspberries (see page 41).

After planting, cut any canes back to 12 in/30cm. In the first

Blackberry 'Loch Ness'

Pear 'Doyenne du Comice'

GROWING TIPS

Peaches are tricky to grow in the garden, needing a lot of extra care. But you might like to try the new dwarf "patio" peaches in a sunny spot. Bring them into a light, cool room from late autumn to the end of May, to protect them from frost and from wet weather, which can spread peach leaf curl on the young leaves.

Fruit trees are sometimes planted as a centerpiece in a lawn. Always leave a 3 ft/90cm circle of bare soil around the trunk, to allow for annual mulching and prevent grass from competing for water and nutrients.

summer, new canes should be trained along the wires, to fruit the following summer. After fruiting, cut them back to ground level and tie in the new set of canes.

Loganberries, with larger, cylindrical fruits, are closely related and can be grown in exactly the same way.

Troubleshooting

Blackberries are healthy plants and not prone to any particular pests or diseases.

Recommended varieties

'Arapatio', 'Chester', 'Illini Hardy', 'Navaho'.

✦ CURRANTS

Currants like a sheltered spot with moisture-retentive soil, in sun or partial shade, and should be spaced 5 ft/1.5 m apart.

In the first winter, cut stems back almost to soil level, so that only one bud is visible. In the second winter, take out any weak or crossing growth. The following summer they will fruit, and the simplest method of pruning once they become fully established is to take out a quarter of

the oldest branches to the base immediately after fruiting. This ensures a constant supply of new fruiting wood.

Troubleshooting

Big bud is caused by a gall mite and is most evident in winter, with some buds much larger and rounder than normal. Pick off and burn them. Serious infestations can cause a virus that drastically reduces crops, and these plants should be destroyed.

Recommended varieties

'Ben Lomond', 'Ben Sarek', 'Boskoop Giant', 'Consort'.

✦ GOOSEBERRIES

Gooseberries are old favorites for pies and jellies, but the eating varieties, bursting with juice and sweetness, are excellent too.

Space plants 5 ft/1.5m apart in a sunny spot. In the first winter, cut out any low-growing shoots, leaving a 6 in/15cm "trunk", and prune the remaining stems back by half. In following winters, remove a few older and crossing branches to keep the center of the bush open and stimulate new growth.

Troubleshooting

Gooseberry sawfly is a caterpillar that strips the leaves in an alarmingly short time. Remove by hand or spray with malathion.

Gooseberry 'Careless'

Recommended varieties

'Careless' (green, cooking), 'Leveller' (green, eating), 'Whinham's Industry' (red, eating and cooking), 'Pixwell' (green, cooking).

✦ PEARS

Eating a ripe pear can be extremely messy, but they're so delicious that you can be excused for forgetting your table manners. Pears need a warm climate and sheltered, sunny location to do well, and can be difficult to grow in very cold regions. And as with apples, you'll need two varieties to ensure cross-pollination.

The two available dwarfing rootstocks are 'Quince C' (approx. 7 ft/2.1m) and 'OH x F 333' (approx. 10 ft/3m). Staking, training, and pruning can be done in the same way as for apples.

Troubleshooting

Scab and brown rot should be dealt with as described for apples. Pear midge lay eggs on flowers and the ensuing maggots cause immature fruits to blacken and fall. Collect and destroy the fruits to help prevent maggots returning to the soil to pupate.

Recommended varieties

'Summer Cusp', 'Harrow Sweet', 'Korean Giant', 'Shin-Li'.

◆ PLUMS

The natural vigor of plums can be cut down to size with a dwarfing rootstock. 'St Julien A' restricts them to around 12 ft/3.6m, and 'Pixy' to a mere 8 ft/2.4m or so. However, the fruit from a tree grown on 'Pixy' rootstock does tend to be smaller than normal.

Plums flower very early, so plant in a warm, sheltered spot where there is least likelihood of frost damage to the flowers. Some plums need another tree for cross-pollination, but those recommended here are self-fertile and can be grown singly. The eating varieties, especially 'Imperial Gage', have a superb, honeyed flavor.

Stake plums as described for apples. No routine pruning is needed, but you can train the tree as it grows, taking out any weak or crossing growths to keep the center open. Always prune in early summer, to reduce the risk of silver leaf disease.

Troubleshooting
Silver leaf is a highly destructive fungus that enters through wounds or pruning cuts. It causes a silvery sheen on leaves and a brown central staining in infected branches. Remove and destroy affected wood, cutting back to healthy, unstained wood. This should be done in the summer months, and the pruning cuts can be painted with a wound sealant, if desired. "False silver leaf" produces similar syptoms but does not stain the wood and is harmless.

Recommended varieties
'Imperial Gage', also known as 'Denniston's Superb' (green, eating), 'Shiro' (yellow, eating), 'Stanley' (blue, eating and cooking), 'Redheart' (red, eating and cooking), 'Fellemberg' (purple, eating and cooking).

◆ RASPBERRIES

Raspberries need a rich, moist soil in sun or part shade. To support the canes, stretch two or three strands of wire between posts, to a height of 5 ft/1.5m. Set plants 18 in/45cm apart and prune each cane to within 10 in/25cm of the ground.

Raspberry 'Autumn Bliss'

Next spring and summer, tie in new canes as they grow. These canes produce fruit the following summer, after which they should be cut back to ground level and fresh canes tied in. Fall-fruiting varieties such as 'Autumn Bliss' and 'Zeva' are an exception – all their canes should be cut back in late winter.

Troubleshooting
Raspberry beetle larvae can infest the fruit. If they are active in your area, spray with malathion when the first berries begin to ripen.

Recommended varieties
'Autumn Bliss', 'Boyne', 'Heritage', 'Latham', 'Royalty'.

◆ STRAWBERRIES

Strawberries are the most eagerly anticipated summer fruits. They need a warm, sunny site that has been generously enriched with well-rotted manure. When planting in pots, tubs, and hanging baskets, use fresh potting mix. Set plants 15 in/40cm apart, leaving 30 in/75cm between rows, with the base of the "crown" (the point from which top growth starts) just below ground level.

In summer, plantlets are formed on long runners, and these should be removed. Fruits can be protected from soil-splash and (to a certain extent) slugs by laying clean, dry straw or special strawberry mats under them. After fruiting, remove any remaining runners, and cut off the older, larger leaves.

Strawberries can crop for three to six years. Discard them once they begin to lose vigor, though you can allow a few runners to root to create a fresh stock of plants. Choose a new planting site and start all over again.

Troubleshooting
Apart from slugs and botrytis (see Pests and Diseases), strawberries are very susceptible to viruses. Be sure to buy virus-free plants. Symptoms vary, but fruiting will deteriorate and as there's no cure, plants should be removed and destroyed.

Recommended varieties
'Garliglow', 'Honeoye', 'Kent', 'Sweet Charlie'.

IDEAS FOR LOW-MAINTENANCE

Colonnade apples grow on a single unbranched stem and need little pruning. Once in a while, they will produce a branch, but this can easily be nipped off.

Alpine strawberries make very pretty ground-cover plants and are especially useful in shady spots. The tiny berries are very flavorful, and you should be able to pick a small handful of fruits each day in the middle of summer. The most widely available variety is 'Fraises des Bois'.

Garden planning and design

Don't let the title put you off. Planning and design is nothing mysterious – it's simply a matter of making the most of your garden's potential, whether you are starting from scratch, taking over an existing yard, or just want to revamp the one you've had for years.

It's a bit like planning to furnish and decorate a room – though in this case the room will actually improve over the years. And as long as you apply a few common-sense rules, you'll end up with a garden that's exactly right for you.

STARTING FROM SCRATCH

Starting with a blank canvas (a yard attached to a new house or a totally neglected, weed-infested plot) is the most exciting challenge of all – your chance to transform one small piece of Mother Earth.

INITIAL PLANNING

First sit down and think what you want from your garden. If you have a young family, it's important to allow for a safe play area such as a lawn, to use tough plants that will survive footballs and games of hide-and-seek, and to avoid potentially dangerous features like a pond or pool. If you also want to use it for entertaining family and friends, you'll need a flat paved area that will comfortably accommodate garden furniture and a barbecue.

How much time do you want to spend working in your yard? Is it for pure relaxation or will you enjoy spending a few hours or more a week working in it? The reason for thinking about this so early in the planning stage is that it helps decide how much space to allocate to different types of plants. Trees, shrubs, and perennial plants, for example, need relatively little care, while a

A strong, simple design is often the most effective. Dwarf boxwood hedges give this garden its structure .

large vegetable plot can be extremely time consuming.

Finally, consider how much money you want to spend. Generally, hard landscaping features (like paths and patios) cost much more than plants and lawns, so you may want to add "hardscape" over time.

Next make a rough plan, marking in the boundary fences or walls, along with the outline of the house and any other fixed features. Then sketch in general areas for borders, patio, paths, lawn, and any other main features. Be practical: a meandering path through the lawn may look pretty, but no one will use it; sheds and

Planning Tips

If you make a mistake and put a plant, especially a tree or shrub, in the wrong spot, don't be afraid to move it – plants of even four or five years old can be moved successfully, especially in fall or early spring. While the soil is moist, dig a planting hole in the new location. Then dig a circle around the plant, excavating as far as you can underneath it. Lift it, retaining as much of the rootball as possible – some damage is inevitable, but very seldom fatal. Transfer it as quickly as possible to the new hole, fill in the soil, and water well. For the next year, keep the plant watered during any dry spells. Older plants can have enormous rootballs, but if your only option is to move them, then at least they have a fighting chance of survival.

When you view the garden from the house or from your favorite sitting area, it's good to have a focal point where the eye can rest for a moment. A beautiful tree, a handsome pot, or even a small statue, carefully sited, can unify the garden design.

Long, narrow gardens are the hardest to design. To avoid the "tunnel" effect, break the space up into a series of "rooms" using plants, trellises, arches, or pergolas. An area of lawn and trees, for instance, will look much more intriguing and inviting if it's first glimpsed through a rose-covered archway or arbor.

If you're nervous about designing your garden, then it may be worthwhile to get professional help. Be careful – some designers are better than others. Ask your friends if they can recommend someone or inquire at your local garden center. When you find a designer you like, visit gardens that the landscaper has worked on rather than looking at sketches and photographs. Or, check through gardening magazines – you may find an article with a landscape plan that you can adapt to your own garden or the name of a landscape architect in your area. Professionals can offer everything from design consultation to complete installation services.

Gravel may seem like a good low-maintenance idea, an inert covering for large expanses of ground. But children love to throw it around, soil infiltrates and weeds begin to sprout, birds can scatter it all over, leaves litter it in fall and are a nuisance to remove, and it should be raked regularly to keep it looking neat.

compost heaps should, ideally, be placed where they'll be hidden from the house; a greenhouse must be in a sunny spot.

And that's really the first stage; it's not worth doing any more planning until you've done some cleaning up outside. This will give you the opportunity of getting to know your garden a bit better and to mull over your initial thoughts.

TAKING A HARD LOOK

If you're pressed for time or money, concentrate your efforts on the back yard and leave the front until later. It's in the back yard that you'll be relaxing, so it deserves to be the priority.

If your garden has been so neglected that you can't see the soil for the weeds, the simplest solution is to destroy them with a nonselective systemic herbicide, as long as you avoid spraying any plants that you want to keep. They're highly effective weedkillers and leave little harmful residue in the soil, so that planting can

A contemplative Oriental statue provides a peaceful focal point in a lushly planted garden.

begin as soon as the weeds have died and been cleared. If you have been "blessed" with really persistent weeds, such as poison ivy or multiflora roses, wait a month or so and give a second application of herbicide to any regrowth.

With a brand new property, the chances are that the builders have left the yard in dreadful condition, even if they've hidden it under a token sprinkling of topsoil. So the first job is to turn the garden over. Dig down one fork's depth and prepare to be horrified by the amount of rubble, wood, and old cement bags that you have to remove. This initial digging also helps to open up the soil, relieving any compaction caused by the heavy construction equipment.

If the soil is poor, improve it by digging in as much organic matter as your wallet and your patience will allow. All is explained in our "Soil Care" chapter. It's hard work, but a wise investment – plants will flourish in well-conditioned soil where otherwise they would have suffered or even died.

While you're out there, take a break from time to time, to note the hot spots and any that remain in shade

Mixing two materials such as brick and gravel makes a real impact and softens the look of a hard surfaced area.

all day – if your rough plan was right, the sitting areas or patio are in the best spots. It's also worth checking whether any part of the garden is particularly windy, so that you can plan for plants to provide shelter.

The final factor to consider before making a more detailed plan is to look at what's beyond your property boundary. Is there an ugly view that you might want to screen off? Or, if you are lucky, a lovely view that you certainly wouldn't want to hide when you plant the garden and may even want to draw attention to.

EVERGREEN ARCHITECHTURE

Never underestimate the importance of evergreen plants in the garden. They provide its basic structure or "bones", making an excellent foil for other plants and flowers in summer and coming into their own in winter, giving shape to the garden when all else is lifeless. Use them wisely – a spire-shaped conifer to mark an intersection, or two of them to frame a vista; in warm regions, sweetly scented

Mexican orange to make a mound of glossy green where it can be seen from the kitchen window; a clipped holly trained as a standard to make a formal accent feature.

Evergreen hedges can be used to define the boundaries of the yard, or even to divide it into compartments. But please, don't plant Leyland cypress. Yes, it provides an almost instant screen, but after that you will either have to keep it pruned

consistently, to restrain its growth, or contend with complaints from the neighbors when the cypress shades out their garden. Also plan for the long term and select evergreens that are low maintenance.

Why not try a yew or hemlock hedge instead? With regular feeding and watering it can grow at a respectable rate, and its dense, dark green foliage always looks incomparably rich and classy.

MAKING THE FINAL PLAN

At this stage, you should prepare a scale plan on graph paper, using a thick dark pen to mark the site boundaries and any features that you want to retain (or have to retain – air conditioning units, for instance, are somewhat permanent). Having made the ground plan, put a piece of tracing paper over it and mark in the proposed layout of patio, paths, lawn, borders, and other major features such as trees. Try out several ideas on separate sheets of tracing paper, then spend time comparing them until you've reached a consensus with the rest of the household.

You can, of course, skip this stage and go straight on to the next, which is to mark out the whole plan on the ground. String and pegs can be used to mark out features like patios, lengths of hose are ideal for showing the position of curved borders and lawns, and large bamboo stakes can be stand-ins for trees. When you've finished fine-tuning the layout, take a look at the layout from an upstairs window, just to check that it looks right from there as well.

SCREENING EYESORES

There are two types of eyesores you may want to screen – your own, and other people's.

In your own yard, you may want to hide the compost heap or an ugly shed. For the shed, you could simply grow an attractive climber on it, or in both instances, a free-standing trellis planted with a climber would do the trick. Ugly walls, too, will benefit from a soft blanket of climbers. Even air conditioning units can be camouflaged by grouping tolerant shrubs around the area.

Eyesores outside the garden are often effectively screened by trees, and it's worth taking a little trouble to site them properly. Find an assistant who can safely handle a long pole (such as two 8 ft/2.4m bamboo stakes lashed together), then stand close to the house and direct the assistant, holding the pole upright, between you and the eyesore. You will eventually hit on just the right spot. It's surprising how a small tree can mask, or at least soften, the view. And don't forget a dense hedge of shrubs – it is ideal not only for screening a view but also for damping noise. Install one at streetside to screen traffic.

This pretty pergola makes a highly decorative screen for that most mundane household object, the trash can.

GETTING GOING

Try to carry out the messiest work first. Generally this is the hardscaping: building the patios and paths. Lay the paths first, so that you have a good surface to work from, and once the patio has been built, you will at least have a place to rest every so often.

If you don't want to tackle planting all at once, fill the rest of the garden with lawn and develop beds and borders as time and money allow. Mowing an extra bit of lawn is a lot less work than keeping empty borders looking neat and weed-free. But try to plant any trees as soon as possible – they'll give instant structure to the garden, and because they often need a couple of years to start growing vigorously, you'll be giving them a head start.

When you do develop the beds and borders, plant the shrubs first – they're the "backbone" of the garden, and it's much easier to decide where they should go and to install them if you haven't already put in the perennials. In the first few years, until your permanent plants fill out, there will inevitably be gaps, so plug them with colorful annuals or other bedding plants in summer.

ASSESSING AN ESTABLISHED GARDEN

If you've moved to a house with an established garden, take at least a year to get to know it before making any changes. Some of the plants may be a bit of a mystery, but most good garden centers would be happy to identify them if you take along a sample of leaves and/or flowers.

Aim simply to keep the garden under control during

> ### IDEAS FOR LOW-MAINTENANCE
>
> *Weeds in paving cracks are a real nuisance, so in addition to making sure that joints in paths and paving are well grouted, lay a down a sheet of plastic or landscaping fabric before paving, so that even the most determined weed can't get a foothold.*
>
> *Incorporating plenty of shrubs and ground-cover plants into your design, and planting as densely as you can, will cut out light from the soil and discourage weeds to a remarkable extent.*
>
> *Paved areas will eventually become dirty, and while you can wash them down with path and patio cleaner, it can be a chore on large expanses. It is much easier and quicker to rent a high-pressure jet washer (more fun, too).*

this period, cutting the lawn to keep it trim and healthy and keeping weeds at bay. Never be too hasty to condemn a plant. That dull shrub may produce a mass of exotic flowers next month. That tangled old apple tree could be properly pruned and soon become a beautiful and productive feature. Both would take years or even decades to replace. So give all plants a year's grace period and if, after that, there are any that you truly dislike, then take them out.

These guidelines apply equally well to your own long-established garden. An excellent and popular way of "previewing" changes is to take a photograph, usually from an upstairs window, enlarge it, then use sheets of clear acetate and erasable markers (from the art supply store) to mark your proposed changes. By superimposing them over the photograph, you'll be able to see quite clearly how they're going to affect the design of the garden. Keep in mind that a garden is never static – it is an ever evolving creation.

Designing by color is a good approach to planting your beds and borders. These shades of red, bronze, and plum-purple combine for a "hot" color scheme.

Growing from seeds and cuttings

There's something magical about growing your own plants from seeds and cuttings. Even for experienced gardeners, there's still a thrill as the seedlings start to emerge, and a great sense of pride when a cutting produces its first new leaves.

It also cuts the cost of gardening dramatically. Most packets of seed are absolute bargains, with the potential to produce lots of plants at just a few cents each. Cuttings are even better, because they're free.

Follow the basic rules and you'll find it one of the most satisfying and rewarding aspects of gardening. Try it – you've nothing to lose except, perhaps, your windowsills.

GROWING FROM SEED

Garden centers sell a good range of the more popular seeds, but for a wider selection, including the best new varieties, send for one of the seed catalogs that are advertised in gardening magazines.

Many plants can be sown outdoors, but others need extra warmth and protection in the early stages, and these should be started indoors – the seed packet will always specify.

DIRECT SEED SOWING

This is the simplest method of sowing seed. Many of the pretty cottage garden plants, such as bachelor's buttons, larkspur, and sweet alyssum, as well as hardy biennials (pansies, forget-me-nots) and most vegetables are grown this way.

Check the recommended sowing time on the seed packet, which will also tell you whether the variety requires a sunny or a partly shady location. Armed with this information, choose a spot in your garden bed, remove any weeds, and fork it over, digging in garden compost or well-rotted manure to give it a boost. Firm the soil by treading on it lightly, and rake it level.

To sow annuals, mark out a series of mini-furrows to the recommended depth and planting distance. Sow the

A well-prepared seedbed, and regular watering in the early stages, are essential for successful germination.

seed in the rows – large seeds are easy to set at the correct spacing, but with smaller ones, just try to distribute them as evenly as possible. Mark the rows with sticks, label them, and water well, using a watering can fitted with a rose.

The seedlings emerge in straight lines, which greatly simplifies weed identification, and although they look rather regimented at first, they'll eventually join together in one dense mass. Any overcrowded clumps should be thinned out by pulling up surplus plants (trying not to disturb those that remain).

Biennials can be treated in the same way, but as they won't flower in the first year, you might want to start them off in a separate nursery bed, transferring them to the desired location in fall.

Vegetables are usually sown in longer rows, which you can mark with string stretched between two pegs. To grow well, they need a richer soil than annuals and biennials, so be sure to work in plenty of well-rotted manure or compost.

All seedlings should be kept well watered, free of weeds, and protected from pests. If cats are a problem (they love the newly turned ground), deter them with netting or a forest of short sticks.

SOWING SEED INDOORS

Many of the most popular summer bedding plants, as well as houseplants and tender crops like tomatoes and peppers, need warmth to start growing, so they should be started indoors, usually in spring.

Seed can be sown in seed trays, but for the average garden, where just a few plants of each variety will be needed, start them off in 3½in/9cm pots. Fill the pot with moist potting or seed-starting mix and firm it down gently. (Never use garden soil, which will become compacted and can harbor disease.) Sow the seeds thinly and cover them to the recommended depth with a further layer of soil. Very small, dustlike seeds may not need to be covered at all, but just pressed in. Water lightly using a watering can fitted with a fine rose.

Label the pots and, if you have a heated propagator, put them in it. If the boiler or warm cupboard is your heat source, cover the pots with a piece of clear plastic or taut plastic wrap, to retain moisture. Most seeds germinate quite happily in a steady temperature of 60-70°F/15-20°C. As soon as the seedlings emerge, place them on a bright windowsill, removing any covering.

When the seedlings are large enough to handle (usually when they've got a couple of pairs of leaves),

SEED GROWING TIPS

To prevent seedlings from becoming leggy while on the windowsill, cover a piece of cardboard with aluminum foil and place it behind the seedlings. The foil reflects light from the window onto the plants, helping them grow much more sturdily.

Very small seeds are easier to sow if mixed with fine sand, which will help you get a more even distribution of the seeds.

Some seeds are more difficult to grow than others. Though it doesn't cost much to try raising them, geraniums, trailing lobelia, begonia, petunia, verbena, and impatiens are among those best left to more experienced gardeners.

Instead of covering pot-grown seeds with potting mix, you can use vermiculite. This lightweight material is sterile, holds warmth and moisture, and improves germination rates.

Separate congested seedlings as soon as they are large enough to handle and transfer them into a tray of fresh soil mix.

transplant them into fresh soil mix in seed trays, cell-packs, or special trays divided into individual cells. Larger seedlings, which will eventually become sizable plants, can be transferred to individual pots up to 3½in/9cm in diameter.

To transplant them, knock the side of the pot to loosen the soil, then gently tip out the contents. Holding a seedling by one of its leaves, ease it away from the group, trying to keep the roots intact. Never handle the stems, which bruise or break very easily.

Using a pencil or dibble, make a hole in the soil mix and insert the seedling. Firm it into place with the pencil, so that the bottom leaves are just clear of the soil, then water them and return them to the windowsill. Keep them moist but not soggy and, after six weeks, start to feed once a week with liquid fertilizer.

If the plants are destined for the garden, it's best to harden them off, because nighttime conditions will be much cooler than they're used to. A couple of weeks beforehand, put them outside in a warm, sheltered spot during the day, bringing them in at night. In the second week, leave them outside all the time, but bring them in if frost or cold temperatures are forecast.

GROWING FROM CUTTINGS

The terms for the different types of cuttings – softwood, semiripe and hardwood – look daunting on paper, but once you've had a good look at the plant that you want to propagate, they'll begin to make sense.

Softwood cuttings: This method, using soft new growth in spring or early summer, gives the quickest results, with cuttings rooting in one to eight weeks.

Using a sharp knife, take cuttings about 4 in/10cm long from the tips of healthy shoots, putting them

TIPS FOR CUTTINGS

Many plants will root in water. So try cuttings from your houseplants, or any garden plant that takes your fancy – ivies, willows, and winter jasmine are especially easy.

When taking clematis cuttings, use the softwood or semiripe method, but always cut halfway between leaf joints, rather than just below. The smaller "species" clematis roots much more readily than the large flowered hybrids.

When chopping up a long stem for hardwood cuttings, make a slanting cut at the base of each portion and a straight cut at the top. That way, you'll be sure to put them in the right way up.

Always remove flowers from cuttings – you need to keep their energy focused on rooting, rather than letting their energy be

straight into a plastic bag to prevent them from drying out. Fill a pot with potting soil and firm it down gently.

Trim each cutting just below a leaf joint, reducing its length to about 3 in/7.5cm. Strip the bottom 2 in/5cm of leaves and dip the base of the cutting in a hormone rooting powder, such as Rootone. Insert the cutting in the soil to half its length, firming the soil around it. Once the pot is full (a 3 in/7.5cm pot can take three or more cuttings), water well.

Softwood cuttings root most quickly in a heated propagator. The alternative is to cover each pot with a clear plastic bag, propping it with sticks so that it sits well away from the leaves and securing it with a rubber band. This can then be placed in a warm bright spot,

Hormone rooting powder encourages root production.

away from direct sunlight. Check often to see if the pots need watering. Once cuttings have rooted and are growing well, they can be separated, replanted in individual pots, and grown uncovered, in a warm, bright place.

Plants to grow from softwood cuttings include geraniums, fuchsias, and most houseplants. Plants such as forsythia, heathers, hydrangea, tree mallow, and potentilla will also root well.

Semiripe cuttings: This is a good method for many shrubs and climbers, with cuttings taken any time from July to early fall.

Side shoots normally yield the best material for semiripe cuttings. You need those that are 4-6 in/10-15cm long and are just beginning to become woody at the base, making your cut just below a leaf joint. Thereafter, semiripe cuttings can be treated in exactly the same way as softwood cuttings, though you don't need to keep them covered.

Good plants to grow from semiripe cuttings are ceanothus, holly, honeysuckle, lavender, mahonia, Mexican orange, pyracantha, rose, viburnum, and weigela.

Hardwood cuttings: This is the slowest method, but by far the simplest, requiring just a spare garden area and a little patience.

Mid– and late fall are the best times for taking hardwood cuttings, and first you should prepare the ground by digging it over until the soil is loose and crumbly. Next make a narrow V-shaped trench about 6 in/15cm deep by inserting your spade and rocking it back and forth. Coarse sand (from the garden center – never builder's sand) stimulates rooting, so place a 1 in/2.5cm layer in the base.

Now choose strong young shoots (those that were produced this year), about the thickness of a pencil. Snip off 9 in/23cm lengths, cutting just below a bud at the base and just above a bud at the top. Dip the base of each cutting in hormone rooting powder, then line them up in the trench 6 in/15cm apart and firm the soil around them. Finally, label and water well. The rooted cuttings can be transplanted to the desired location in the garden the following fall.

Some of the more popular plants easily propagated by hardwood cuttings are buddleia, cotoneaster, forsythia, honeysuckle, jasmine, ivy, mock orange, roses, and spirea – but it's worth trying with any woody plant.

Hanging baskets and window boxes

Put a hanging basket bursting with flowers by the front door or place a newly planted window box on a ledge and an amazing transformation takes place. The whole area immediately brightens up and feels warmer and more welcoming. They are among the easiest ways to perk up your property.

Although hanging baskets and window boxes are by no means an essential part of gardening, like all life's frivolities they're guaranteed to lift the heart and bring a smile to your face.

GROWING SUCCESS

They are, admittedly, time-consuming to look after – they need watering, feeding, and deadheading, but try to spare the time for just one or two. They'll keep you cheerful for months on end.

HANGING BASKETS

Hanging baskets are available in a range of shapes and sizes, but the round wire basket is still the traditional favorite. These can be planted around the sides as well as the top, so that you can cram in a mass of plants for a really bold, lush display.

They need to be lined, of course, to retain the soil mix, and fresh green sphagnum moss blends in best with the plants, though there's also a synthetic moss substitute that looks almost like the real thing. Wool, fiber, and rigid liners are also available, but they're very unattractive – planting is easier, but you'll probably regret buying them.

Plastic baskets are undoubtedly easier to plant, because they don't need lining. Easier to care for too, since they don't dry out as quickly and some versions even have built-in self-watering devices. But somehow, even when in full flower, they never look quite as charming as the wire baskets.

WINDOW BOXES

Garden centers sell a wide range of window boxes in clay, wood, or plastic. Their relative merits are discussed in "Container Gardening" (see page 29), but there are some specific points worth considering, whichever you choose.

Larger, deeper boxes hold more soil and need less frequent watering. However, a large box placed in front of a small window can block lots of daylight, so you'll probably have to compromise. One of the best solutions is to position and support the box just below the window ledge, allowing plenty of room for plant growth, especially if you have casement windows.

All shades of pink, from the palest to deep rose, make this a wonderfully harmonious window-box planting.

PLANTING AND CARING FOR A SUMMER BASKET

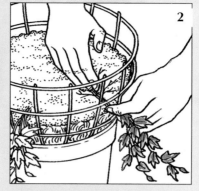

Planting a wire hanging basket is labor intensive but not difficult, and the layered planting produces the most spectacular results.

• Place the basket on top of a bucket to keep it steady during planting. Line the bottom with a 1 in/2.5cm layer of sphagnum moss (1).

• Use edging lobelia or something similar as your "base" plant to form a full globe of background color, setting the plants 3 in/7.5cm apart in a circle around the edges (2). Work from the inside, carefully pushing the leaves through the gaps in the basket and resting the roots on the moss.

• Add another layer of moss around the side of the basket, to the half-way mark. Plant a second circle of lobelia, positioning it so that it doesn't overhang the plants of the first circle. Using potting soil, fill in around the rootballs of the plants and firm gently.

• Make a third layer of moss and plants, top up with soil mix, then moss the basket to the rim.

• Next plant the top of the basket, positioning the tallest upright plant (such as a geranium) in the center, smaller upright plants around it (3), and trailing plants at the edges. (Don't worry about cramming – the best baskets have plenty of plants.)

• Fill in any gaps with soil mix, water thoroughly, and finally hang the basket in position on a strong, well-secured bracket.

• From then onward, the key to a long-lasting display is regular watering, feeding, and deadheading. Watering is the most time-consuming chore once the weather warms up and plants are growing vigorously. So check the basket every day and try to water in the early morning or in the cool of the evening. Instead of lifting a heavy watering can, use a 1 liter plastic bottle, which contains just about the right amount of water. Even easier, use a spraying wand on the hose.

Feeding won't be necessary for the first six weeks, but thereafter, feed once a week with a high-potassium fertilizer such as liquid tomato food or a balanced food like 5-10-5. Deadheading, the regular removal of faded blooms, not only keeps the basket looking good, it also prevents the plants from going to seed and ceasing to flower.

PLANTING A WINDOW BOX

Planting a window box is just like planting any other container. It's essential to have drainage holes in the bottom, so make some if necessary. Add 2 in/5cm of drainage material, such as broken clay pots or foam packing "peanuts", then fill with potting soil. Plant taller-growing varieties at the back, then smaller and trailing plants at the front and sides.

Firm the soil, adding more if needed, water well, and make sure the box is secure – you don't want it falling off in a gust of wind. To prolong the life of a wooden window box, insert a plastic liner.

Aftercare is the same as for hanging baskets, though it's unlikely you'll have to water every day. Just check regularly in hot, dry weather.

Making the most of
Summer Color

Most people mix lots of different plants and flower colors in the same basket or box, and it can look lovely. But you'll get some even better effects if you're slightly more selective. Experiment with simple color schemes – warm colors like gold, orange, and red look great together, as do cool blues and whites. Or go for a blend of similar colors, for instance white, pale pink, and rose pink. If you're feeling more adventurous, the most striking schemes are based on really strong contrasts like yellow with purple, blue with orange, and red with green.

FLOWERING PLANTS

Flowering plants are the obvious first choice for boxes and baskets, but there are some very pretty foliage plants that will add an extra splash of color. Look out, in particular, for varieties with bronze, gold, or white-variegated leaves. And silver-leaved plants like dusty miller and helichrysum blend beautifully with pink, white, or blue flowers.

It's always difficult to judge which plants will look good together, but one of the easiest ways is to wander around the garden center, gathering up all the plants you think you might like and putting them in a window box or basket that is roughly the same size as the one you've got at home. If one plant or color doesn't fit your scheme, then keep changing until you've got the perfect combination.

Of course, you don't have to confine yourself to bedding plants – it's fun to experiment with other

The rich, hot colors of geraniums and verbena, teamed with dark blue lobelia, make a tremendous impact.

types of plants as well. One of the prettiest baskets we've ever seen was crammed full of colorful herbs, a riot of golden marjoram, silver thyme, purple sage, daisy-flowered chamomile, and a few bright nasturtiums with their big, lily pad-like leaves.

Another subtle but effective combination can be achieved with vegetables, which are often very ornamental and colorful. Plant a mix of frilly red-leaved lettuces along with ruby chard and radicchio. In cold climates, plant the box with red, pink, and white ornamental cabbages in late summer.

Making the most of
Winter Color

At the end of summer, your plants will start to fade (and who can blame them – they must be exhausted). But don't just empty the basket and leave it in the shed to hibernate – where winters are not too cold, give it a new lease on life.

From September onwards, garden centers sell a range of small evergreens, such as miniature conifers, which are ideal as replacements for the taller bedding plants in the center of the basket. Around these, plant colorful heathers, and winter-flowering pansies; and to give it some real pizazz for spring, don't forget to pop in some dwarf bulbs. As a finishing touch, plant variegated trailing ivy around the edges.

The basket will look lovely from fall through late spring and, as a bonus, you'll find it needs far less care than a summer basket. There's no need to feed it – just give it an occasional watering if it's necessary over winter, then water more regularly in spring as the weather warms up.

Don't give up on your window boxes either. One of the simplest schemes is a mass of winter-flowering pansies (it's particularly effective if they're all the same color) underplanted with bulbs such as dwarf narcissus or species tulips. To add height put in some small evergreens – golden-leaved forms are especially good since they will look bright and cheerful even in the depths of winter.

In this wall basket lined with old fern fronds, hellebores are planted with snowdrops and cyclamen to bring color and cheer to a mild-climate garden, in late winter.

SITING AND SECURITY

A hanging basket, fully planted and well watered, can be very heavy, so it's important that the bracket is strong enough to take the weight and is securely fastened to the wall.

Depending on your choice of plants, baskets can be hung in most locations, but they're never very successful in windy spots. Most will withstand the occasional buffeting, but not constant wear and tear. Sheltered positions really are the best.

Window boxes, too, can be extremely heavy and must be attached securely in place. On sills that slope forwards, put small wedges under the front of the box to keep it level and attach metal brackets to the sides of the window recess or to the sill itself to prevent the box from slipping forwards.

It's well worth placing a plastic tray under the window box to stop excess water from running down the side of the building. And if you're a high-rise gardener, water won't get dripped on your neighbors.

Top Ten Plants for Hanging Baskets and Window Boxes

Tuberous begonias

Swan river daisy with meadow foam

✦ BEGONIAS
The fibrous-rooted semperflorens varieties are superb, with a neat, rounded habit, glossy green or dark bronze foliage, and red, white, or pink flowers all summer. Tuberous begonias are much larger (to 2 ft/ 60 cm) and more flamboyant, with large double flowers in startlingly electric colors; in our opinion, the upright varieties are much better than the trailing forms. Begonias will grow in sun or shade.

✦ BIDENS
A wonderfully vigorous trailing plant with ferny leaves and masses of starry gold flowers through summer. It can become slightly untidy and may need occasional trimming to keep it under control. One of its many virtues is that it's remarkably tough and can withstand being dried out for a few days – once watered it will start

growing again as if nothing had happened. Best in a sunny spot.

✦ *BRACHYCOME* (Swan river daisy)
This bushy 10 in/25cm plant is a real gem in a sunny, sheltered spot, making mounds of finely cut leaves studded with tiny daisy flowers. The best of the colors is the pale purple, almost blue, shade – the pinks and whites can look somewhat rather washed out in sun. In addition to being extremely pretty, the flowers are invaluable in hanging baskets because they close up when thirsty – a useful reminder to water.

Bidens with trailing helichrysum

PLANTING TIPS

Baskets and boxes can be successful in light shade, but you need to be more careful in the plants you choose. Impatiens, begonias, fuchsias, flowering tobacco, and variegated ivies are particularly good.

It can be difficult to keep a hanging basket steady while planting it. Instead of placing it on a flat surface, set the basket atop an empty bucket.

Draw the eye beyond the bounds of the basket or box by planting in all planes. Use a tall, columnar plant to create height, bushy plants to suggest a sense of depth, and trailing plants to add length.

Don't forget that baskets and boxes should never be placed outdoors until all danger of frost has passed. If you want to get a head start, plant the containers early and place them in a light, frost-free spot or under artificial lights.

Impatiens

◆ IMPATIENS

These put on a wonderful display whatever the weather. They flower from early summer to first frosts, and are available in a range of colors. Look for the 'Super Elfin' series, which are more compact and therefore better suited to baskets and boxes. Best in light shade, they can also tolerate a bit of neglect.

◆ GERANIUM (*Pelargonium*)

This classic for sunny locations looks superb all summer. Use the upright varieties in the center of the basket or back of the window box and plant trailing forms at the edge. For a change from the globelike flower heads, try the wispier ivy-leaved geraniums – they will spill over the sides of baskets and window boxes with colorful, airy sprays of flowers that are delicately veined. Geraniums are remarkably tough and soon bounce back if you forget to water them. But you will need to deadhead religiously to ensure a floral display.

◆ HELICHRYSUM PETIOLARE

These spreading, trailing foliage plants add invaluable structure as well as attractive leaf color to planting combinations. The soft, felted leaves come in a variety of colors, but the silvery gray is the best known (the small-leaved compact form is very good). Yellow and variegated helichrysums are also excellent. Best in sunny locations, they are drought tolerant.

◆ PANSY

Winter– and spring-flowering pansies are best; don't bother with the summer varieties, which suffer badly if you forget to water them. Available in a superb range of colors, they make striking displays. Among the most charming are the tiny Princess hybrids violas, best grown in boxes and baskets close to the house where you can enjoy their cheerful faces in close-up.

Geraniums

Pansies

Petunias

✦ PETUNIA

Best in sunny locations, petunias will provide a fine display, except in the wettest summers. The 'Surfinia' hybrids are particularly splendid, but incredibly vigorous. Three plants will fill a 14 in/35cm basket on their own and trail as much as 4 ft/1.2m, spreading out almost as wide. The new compact 'Junior' types are much less domineering, however. All petunias need to be deadheaded regularly to ensure continuous flowering.

✦ SMALL EVERGREENS

Widely available in garden centers, these are invaluable for winter and spring displays. Dwarf or slow-growing conifers, golden-leaved *Euonymus fortunei* 'Emerald 'n' Gold' or white variegated *E. f.* 'Silver Queen', and small skimmias make good centerpieces and can be planted in the garden when containers are needed for summer bedding. Winter-flowering heathers, as well as those with colorful foliage, provide an excellent contrast in the foreground, and small variegated ivies can be planted around the edges.

✦ VERBENA

Available in trailing, upright, and dwarf form, spicily scented verbenas flower from early summer until first frost. They are lovely, dainty plants that really earn their keep, offering a continuous succession of pincushion clusters of flowers. Some can be prone to mildew, but among the resistant cultivars are soft pink 'Silver Anne', and cerise pink 'Sissinghurst'.

Verbena *'Amethyst'*

IDEAS FOR LOW-MAINTENANCE

A typical hanging basket needs about 1 quart of water per day in summer (and twice a day in very hot weather). If you have lots of baskets, it's worth considering a few tricks to cut down the time spent on watering:

• *The bigger the basket you plant, the less watering it will need. A 14 in/35cm basket holds 50 percent more soil mix than a 12 in/30cm basket, and this extra volume mix helps conserve water.*

• *Adding water-retaining crystals (hydrogel) to the potting mix when planting can greatly reduce the frequency of watering. Mix the dry granules (available at garden centers) with water and stir to make a thick gel. When incorporated into the soil mix, they release water to the plants as needed. But a word of warning – they will also swell if swallowed, so keep the crystals away from children.*

• *Position the basket in a spot that's sheltered from drying winds and, if possible, where it gets some shade from the full blaze of midday sun.*

Some plants are much more tolerant of neglect than others. Some that recover well if you've forgotten to water them include: begonias, swan river daisy, impatiens, cineraria, felicia, helichrysum, gazania, French marigolds, nasturtiums, petunias, and verbena. The toughest of them all are bidens and geraniums. Fuchsias in particular are a nightmare if neglected, so they should preferably not be used by low maintenance gardeners.

Hanging baskets and window boxes must be fed regularly during the summer, or plants will run out of gas and stop flowering. Rather than using liquid food once a week, add slow-release fertilizer

Hardy perennials

Hardy perennial *is a handy catch-all term for a huge range of plants, but basically it means any long-lived frostproof plant that isn't a tree or shrub.*

Stately delphiniums are the essence of the summer garden.

The major group is the flowering herbaceous perennials – those wonderful plants that fill the spring and summer borders with color and die back to the ground in winter. But there are also others, like grasses and ferns, that we grow for the beauty of their foliage.

Long-lived, trouble-free, increasing in beauty year by year, perennials give enormous pleasure in return for relatively little effort.

GROWING SUCCESS

Most hardy perennials will be with you for a long time, so it's worth giving them a hearty welcome by preparing the ground well before planting. Fork it over to loosen it and mix in plenty of organic matter, such as compost or well-rotted manure.

Water your plants before setting them in the ground at the same level as they were in the pot, firming the soil around them. Water again and keep watering for the first few weeks if the weather is dry. They don't need any regular feeding, but a spring boost of an all-purpose balanced fertilizer, such as 5-10-5, and a layer of organic mulch will be gratefully received.

Exploit the wonderful diversity of hosta leaf shapes, colors, and forms.

Flowering plants can be kept looking neat by deadheading (removing faded flowerheads), and some will reward you with a second, smaller flush of bloom. Most perennials die back in winter, and the old growth can be cut down to ground level in late fall.

LEAFY PERENNIALS

Although we tend to think of hardy perennials in terms of flowery summer borders, there are some that have a lot to offer with the beauty of their foliage. The large, sculpted leaves of hostas make them an obvious first choice. There are other plants, however, that are easy to overlook at first glance but will become favorites.

Pulmonaria (lungwort), despite the name, is a pretty little plant. After the spring display of blue, white, or pink flowers, the leaves take over, forming dense, silver-splashed rosettes that look their best in a shady spot in damp soil.

For the front of a sunny border, try low-growing **lamb's ears** *(Stachys byzantina)*; the silvery leaves are thickly felted, and the temptation to stroke them is irresistible. The tall spikes of purple flower are a bonus.

Investigate the **grasses**, too. Most of the fine-leaved fescues are an intense silver-blue, especially in a sunny spot, and grow into graceful mounds. And there's a lovely golden grass worth tracking down, *Milium effusum* 'Aureum' (Bowles' golden grass); in a moist soil it makes an arching fountain of soft leaves that will light up a shady spot, and it seeds itself readily.

Finally, there are **ferns**, which seem to be creeping back into fashion. Though normally associated with moist conditions, many will thrive in drier soil, so always check the growing instructions. One of the prettiest of the smaller types is the soft shield fern *(Polystichum setiferum* and its cultivars*)*, which bears lacy fronds of fresh green. And if it's a giant you want, try *Osmunda regalis*, the royal fern, which can reach 5 ft/1.3m in cultivation.

A combination of contrasting leaf sizes, forms, and textures makes a long-lasting display.

DIVISION

Many hardy perennials will spread into quite substantial clumps, and after three or four years the center of the clump may become overcrowded or die out and produce fewer flowers. So to rejuvenate them, and increase your stock, divide them.

The best times to do this is in fall (when they'll be starting to go dormant) or early spring (when they'll be eager to start growing). Water the plants if the soil is dry, then dig around them with a fork and lift the whole clump, taking as much of the root as possible.

This is where it may become tricky, because while some will separate into plantlets simply by teasing them apart, others are so woody that you may have to chop through them with a spade, machete, or a sharp knife. It sounds brutal, but as long as each portion has a reasonable number of roots attached, it should be all right. Pick the best, most vigorous plantlets and replant them at the original depth – they'll soon develop.

But just a word of warning: some perennials are poisonous or have irritant sap, so if in doubt, always wear gloves and try not to get plant juices on your skin.

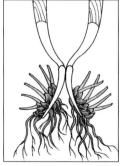

Two forks back to back can be used to pry plant clumps apart.

The resulting smaller clumps can usually be divided by hand.

Replant clumps in well-prepared soil and water them in thoroughly.

Making the most of Peonies

Peonies are popular hardy perennials, with large, luscious heads of single or ruffled double flowers in all shades from deep red to pure white. Their season is all too short – just a few weeks in early summer – but we do urge you to grow them; you'll carry the memory of those sumptuous flowers all year.

But, like all great beauties, peonies should be cherished and given some extra attention to keep them at their loveliest. They must have a sunny, well-drained spot, liberally enriched with organic matter, and it's vital that you plant them at the right depth – too deep and they'll refuse to flower. The

Paeonia lactiflora *'Bowl of Beauty'*

crown (the point from which top growth starts) should be no more than 1 in/ 2.5cm below ground level.

The flowers of the double cultivars are so full and heavy that they can droop, bending over so far that they touch the ground unless you support them. "Gro-thru" plant supports are ideal, allowing each flower stem to be individually spaced, but you could compromise with a dense network of twiggy sticks or stake individual stems with bamboo.

When it comes to mulch, keep it at a respectful distance from the stems – about 3 in/7.5cm – as it can harbor pests and diseases. Also be sure not to

dump the mulch over the plant – just place it on the ground.

Finally, put up a "do not disturb" sign; they hate to be moved. If you're forced to do so, expect few flowers for a year or more.

Peonies are amazingly long-lived. They can last for 50 years and more, and if you treat them with the respect they deserve, they'll never look a day over 25.

LONG-LASTING COLOR

The bold colors of ruby penstemon and purple salvia are toned down by a soft pink rose.

Hardy perennials allow numerous opportunities for playing with color. If you want to be really bold, plant a whole group of the "hot" colors – red-orange *Kniphofia* (red-hot poker), scarlet oriental poppies, ruby-flowered sedums, flaming orange crocosmia (montbretia), golden achillea (yarrow), and rudbeckia (black-eyed Susan), gaily striped gaillardias, crimson penstemons, and rich orange, red, or yellow helianthemums. This color combination may sound terribly gaudy, but if you tone it down with a few foliage plants, you can achieve some wonderful effects.

For a more subtle, restful look, try a quieter design in the tried-and-true formula of pink, white, and blue. *Nepeta* (catmint) gives a long-lasting haze of soft blue, as does the low-growing scabious 'Butterfly Blue'. Pink can be provided by hardy geraniums, peonies, astilbes, and (appropriately enough) the garden pinks – those sweetly clove-scented varieties of dianthus. For white, add a mist of tall baby's breath, groups of Shasta daisies, white forms of *Anemone* × *hybrida*, white bell-flowers, and *Boltonia* 'Snowbank'. Delphiniums, of course, come conveniently in all three colors.

Top Ten Hardy Perennials

• *ALCHEMILLA MOLLIS* (Lady's mantle) Zones 3-9

A real charmer – soft green scalloped leaves and airy plumes of acid-yellow flowers in early summer, to 18 in/45cm. They seed freely and will establish in all sorts of nooks and crannies. Cut them back almost to ground level when the foliage becomes shabby for a fresh show of

PLANTING TIPS

Hardy perennials always look best planted in groups of three or five. An expensive operation, but you could always buy one plant and divide it after a couple of years. And watch for larger plants at garden centers – very often they're so mature that they can be split up before planting.

The lush spring growth of many hardy perennials is irresistible to slugs. So if these pests are prevalent in your area, don't plant hostas, delphiniums, and other slug favorites.

If you've got a damp low, spot in the yard, turn it into a bog garden. There are a number of hardy perennials that will thrive in moist soil, including daylily, filipendula, Japanese primrose, monkey flower, bee balm, rodgersia, purple loosestrife, and astilbe.

If you want something exotic in your perennial garden, plant eryngiums (sea hollies). These are spring, prickly plants in steely silver and blue-purple, with a metallic sheen to the leaves and flowers. They make excellent dried flowers or can be left uncut through winter as dramatic architectural skeletons.

tender young leaves and perhaps a sprinkling of flowers. Lady's mantle is completely pest- and disease-free and grows anywhere and everywhere, but is especially good to soften the edges of paths and patios.

• *CAMPANULA* (Bellflower) Zones 3-9

Bellflowers are one of the easiest cottage-garden flowers, needing only well-drained soil, in sun or partial shade. The low-growing *C. carpatica*, is lovely for the front of the border, with wide, upturned blue or white flowers in late spring to summer. Try *C. persicifolia* – tall spikes of delicate white or blue flower to 3 ft/90cm on wiry stems throughout the summer. And most striking of all, but not as hardy, *C. lactiflora*, with huge heads of milky-blue bells to 4 ft/1.2m in summer. Any, and every, bellflower is worth growing.

• *CROCOSMIA* (Montbretia) Zones 5-9

One of the joys of late summer, with arching stems of blazing orange-red flowers above spearlike leaves. One of the most outstanding is 'Lucifer', the flame-orange flowers topping 3ft/90cm; of the slightly shorter

Euphorbia polychroma

varieties, 'Fireking' and burnt-orange 'Emberglow' are excellent. Plants eventually form dense stands, which can be lifted and divided with a sharp spade. Give crocosmias a sunny location in well-drained soil. Pest- and disease-free, these are easy, showy plants for anyone to grow.

• DELPHINIUM Zones 3-8

Classic midsummer flowers that soar to 6 ft/1.8m and are breathtaking, but they require some care. Give them a rich soil in a sunny, sheltered spot and protect the emerging shoots and young foliage from slugs in spring. To keep them from bending, stake the stems from an early stage, tying them in as they grow. Deadhead to the base of the flower spikes as soon as they fade to encourage a second, smaller blooming. Be extra generous when mulching in spring. Just a note: Pacific Hybrid/Giant delphiniums are very short-lived, so consider treating them as annuals.

• EUPHORBIA Zones 8-10

Euphorbias are remarkably varied, and the most striking is *E. wulfenii*, with bottlebrush stems of gray-green leaves topped by cylindrical heads of long-lasting sulphur-yellow flower bracts in spring, to 3 ft/90cm. In contrast, the much hardier *E. polychroma* is a neatly domed plant, to 18 in/45cm, with acid yellow bracts. Most euphorbias do best in sun, in any ordinary soil. For ground cover in difficult locations use *E. robbiae*, with handsome dark green leaves; it spreads even in the driest shade. Take care when cutting out flowered stems – the sap is a severe irritant.

Geranium *'Johnson's Blue'*

◆ GERANIUM Zones 5-10

Good tempered, undemanding and pest- and disease-free, hardy geraniums will grow almost anywhere, for anyone. They are wonderful as ground covers and bloom profusely with successions of delightful small flowers. Colors range from white through pink to violet and deep purple, and some blossoms are prettily veined, with a contrasting central eye. For dry shade, use the pink *G. macrorrhizum*. Other excellent geraniums include *G.* x *oxonianum* 'A.T. Johnson', with long-lasting silvery pink flowers, and *G.* 'Johnson's Blue', with soft blue-violet blooms. Cut back hard after flowering – there's often a repeat performance.

◆ HELLEBORUS Zones 3-9

For winter and early spring flowers hellebores are a must. The true Christmas rose, *H. niger*, can be tricky, but the less demanding *H. orientalis* hybrids, flowering in early spring, are equally lovely and have a good color range from white to deep plum. To show off the low-growing flowers, cut out the older leaves and surround the plant with a layer of shredded bark to prevent soil splashes. Hellebores enjoy partial shade and a fertile, moisture-retentive (but not waterlogged) soil.

◆ HOSTA Zones 3-9

Hostas are the most architectural of all herbaceous plants, forming wide rosettes of sculpted leaves. *H. sieboldiana elegans* is the noblest of them all – with large, deeply ribbed blue-gray leaves up to 1 ft/30cm across. The *H. fortunei* varieties are smaller, with some excellent variegated forms. Hostas can be used almost anywhere in the garden, but the soil must be reasonably fertile. They'll grow best in partial shade, and the only situation they really dislike is a hot, dry spot. They do need protection from slugs or they'll be badly tattered by midsummer.

◆ PAEONIA (Peony) Zones 2-9

Peonies appear in early summer and, except for roses, there's nothing that can match them. They're often sold simply as "red", "white", and so on, but if you get the chance to pick out named cultivars, look for the beautiful doubles. 'Duchesse de Nemours' is a ruffled globe of white, 'Felix Crousse' a rich crimson red, and 'Sarah Bernhardt'

Hellebore flowers

apple blossom pink – and all are deliciously scented. Peonies grow to around 3 ft/90cm, and the leaves remain an attractive feature throughout summer. Once established they'll live for many years, and if you follow the guidelines in "Making the most of Peonies" you won't go far wrong.

◆ PHLOX PANICULATA Zones 3-9

One of the old faithfuls of the flower border, making increasingly larger stands of 3 ft/90cm stems, topped with clusters of flowers from summer through early fall. It's a tough, undemanding plant in sun or partial shade and a fertile soil. In soils that tend to dry out, you'll find that it droops and will need extra water. Dry soil also makes the plants more vulnerable to mildew. The colors are wonderful, from pure white to scarlet, mauve, and cerise. To increase your stocks, just lift and divide them in early fall or spring, replanting the best portions.

IDEAS FOR LOW-MAINTENANCE

Many hardy perennials make excellent ground cover, either because of their dense ground-hugging leaf cover or because they send out an impenetrable mat of roots close to the surface. Lady's mantle, ajuga, hostas, and geraniums are all particularly good.

*Creeping Jenny (*Lysimachia nummularia*) is an instant charmer with its buttercup flowers, but it's quite invasive and may have to be pulled up. So avoid planting it in heavy soils, where the underground stems and tenacious roots will be almost impossible to remove completely.*

Herbs

Herbs are such virtuous plants: easy to please, pest- and disease-free, decorative, aromatic, and attractive to bees and butterflies. And most important of all, delicious – freshly picked herbs can transform a dish from the mediocre to the sublime. A little tarragon inside the chicken as it roasts, a sprig of rosemary with lamb, a sprinkle of basil on sliced tomatoes – wonderful.

Standard bay trees flank a collection of herbs grown in pots.

Throw away those little jars of tired dried leaves, and invest in the real thing – living plants full of freshness, aroma, and flavor.

GROWING SUCCESS

Almost without exception, herbs are ridiculously easy to grow. Starting from seed is the cheapest option, and many specialist herb catalogs offer an astonishing range of choices. But if you want an instant plant, garden centers are becoming much more adventurous, and you should find a good selection.

Full sun and a well-drained soil suits most herbs best, but a few (parsley, mint, chervil, lovage, and sorrel) can be grown in partial shade and moist (but not soggy) soil. There's generally no need to enrich the soil before planting, since herbs are not "hungry" plants, but do turn it over with a fork to improve drainage. Heavy clay soils can be opened up by digging in plenty of gypsum (calcium sulfate) and organic matter, such as compost or well-rotted manure. In pots, use a free-draining soil mix.

Set your plants at the same level as they were in the pot and water well. Keep them watered for the first few weeks if the weather is dry, but thereafter they need very little attention. Perennial herbs die down in winter, and the old growth can be cut back to ground level in fall.

Most herbs are perfectly hardy and will live for many years, though a handful (such as chervil, coriander, and dill) are annuals, which grow, flower, and die in one season and will need to be replaced each spring. Parsley, too, is best grown fresh each year. The only really frost-sensitive herb that you're likely to meet is basil. Rosemary is hardy only to zone 7.

HERB PLANTINGS

An herb garden is a wonderful place – soft colors, rich scents, and the drone of contented bees. Experimenting with foliage contrasts is great fun – spires of rosemary with spiky clumps of chives; smoky wisps of fennel, chervil, and dill with dense mats of thyme; fronds of bright green parsley with a ferny haze of sweet cicely. Try planting them in patterns, between the spokes of an old cartwheel, for instance – though only the neater, less rampant herbs such as basil should be used in such a confined space. You can also divide them into small beds edged with weathered brick; bricks and herbs are a lovely combination.

That's the ideal, of course, but if you can't spare the space for a whole herb plot, plant them in beds and borders. Grow thyme close to paths where you'll brush past and release the scent. Edge a formal border with a line of chives. Plant fennel as a foil for roses.

In small gardens, grow herbs in pots in a sunny spot. Clay pots, though more expensive than plastic, always look good with herbs, and you can cluster them together to make a miniature herb garden.

To harvest herbs, gather them on a warm, dry day, preferably before they are in full flower, and hang them upside down in small bunches in a warm place – an attic is ideal. Once they're thoroughly brittle, crumble them up and put them in jars. Dark glass jars are best, or keep clear jars in a cabinet to exclude light.

Top Ten Essential Herbs

◆ BASIL

Basil is a delicate herb, but so delicious that it's worth the extra care. A tender annual, it resents the cold, so give it a sunny, sheltered spot. It does well in pots outdoors or in the greenhouse, where the powerful aroma from the leaves will banish whitefly, or on a bright windowsill indoors. Besides the plain green forms of basil, look for the attractive purple and fancy-leaved varieties. Pinch out the growing tips to keep plants bushy and remove any flowers.

◆ CHIVES

These reed-leaved members of the onion family are a cinch, growing well for even the most neglectful gardener. All they ask is ordinary garden soil and sun or partial shade. Two close relatives are the Egyptian and Welsh onions – harder to find,

Chives

but equally tough. These two have leaves that are fat and tubular and a stronger flavor. The Egyptian has the extraordinary habit of producing tiny onion bulbs from its flowerheads.

◆ FENNEL

Anise-flavored fennel is a beautiful herb with plumes of feathery foliage to a height of 4 ft/1.2m. Any soil will suit it, in full sun. In addition to their culinary virtues, the filigree leaves are extremely pretty in flower arrangements, especially if you grow the bronze-purple form. Its close relation, Florence fennel, is an annual vegetable, valued for the flavorful 'bulb' at the base.

◆ MARJORAM

Marjoram, also known as oregano, has a nicely rounded flavor; a bit like thyme, but smoother. Sweet marjoram (*Origanum majorana*) should be grown as an annual, so for perennial pleasure you'll need oregano (*Origanum vulgare*). This makes spreading mounds of soft,

small leaves, and the golden form, 'Aureum' really lights up the garden. Marjoram needs sun and a well-drained soil, plus an annual trim after flowering.

◆ MINT

Mint has a uniquely clean, refreshing flavor, and the manners of a thug, spreading from runners and overwhelming anything in its path. So keep it caged. Growing it in pots is an ideal solution, but in the garden you can plant it in bottomless containers

Chives

Silver-variegated thyme

Oregano

PLANTING TIPS

For a winter supply of fresh herbs like chives, parsley, mint, tarragon, or thyme, transfer them into pots in early August, cut them back, and bring them indoors before the first frosts. Placed on a light windowsill, they'll keep growing for months on end.

Bay laurel grows well in pots, and looks very handsome by a doorway or on a terrace. Try training yours into a pyramid, trimming the tree to shape while it's growing vigorously in summer. In cold climates, and in severe weather, protect bays from frost damage by draping them with landscape fabric or bring them indoors.

sunk into the ground. Mint prefers a moist soil, in sun or partial shade. Apple mint and spearmint have the finest flavor, but look for decorative variegated forms such as the white-blotched pineapple mint.

✦ PARSLEY

Although fresh parsley is always available at the grocery store, grow your own crop from seed if you want a good supply. To germinate and flourish, parsley must have a moist, fertile soil in sun or partial shade. So add plenty of organic matter before sowing and keep the seedbed well watered until the seed has germinated. Technically, parsley is a biennial, but it's never as good in the second year, so sow fresh seed each spring. Flat-leaved Italian parsley has

the best flavor, but curly-leaved parsley is quite ornamental.

✦ ROSEMARY

With its spiky leaves, soft blue flowers, and aromatic scent, rosemary is a valuable evergreen shrub, though it is not reliably hardy in colder areas. It needs well-drained soil and a sunny, sheltered location. In addition to the common forms, look for the tall, vigorous 'Miss Jessop's Upright' and the lovely arching 'Severn Sea'. To keep plants neat and bushy, cut all growths back by half each year, in early spring or before.

✦ SAGE

In addition to its culinary merits, sage is another useful garden shrub – evergreen, hardy to zone 6, and attractively shaped. The common form has gray-green leaves, but there are also gold-splotched and purple-leaved forms that are excellent for a mixed border and equally tasty. 'Tricolor', splashed with pink and white, is especially attractive but not as hardy as the rest. Give sage a sunny, well-drained soil and cut back any straggly branches in spring to keep it bushy.

✦ TARRAGON

The tarragon that you grow from seed is Russian and not nearly as good as French tarragon, which can only be bought as plants. If you know someone who grows it, ask for a few of the runners that form around the plant, and grow them in your own

> ## IDEAS FOR LOW-MAINTENANCE
>
> *Herbs, by their very nature, are low-maintenance plants – they're virtually immune to pests and diseases and positively dislike it when they are overwatered or overfed.*
>
> *Thyme, marjoram, and sage, with their dense, spreading habit, are in- valuable ground-cover plants and will soon smother out all but the most persistent weeds. Lemon balm, an aromatic herb, will do the same job, but seeds itself freely, so snip off the flowers – they're pretty insignificant anyway.*
>
> *For an aromatic informal hedge, use rosemary, planted at 3 ft/90cm intervals. In warmer climates, the pretty blue flowers are produced almost continuously, and plants need to be trimmed only once a year, in spring, to prevent them from becoming too straggly.*

garden. Tarragon does best in light soils, in sun. In colder regions, lift a plant or two and put them in pots to overwinter indoors.

✦ THYME

Of all the herbs, thyme is perhaps the most valued as a garden plant. It forms low, spreading mounds with dainty, tiny leaves that are plain green or variegated in gold or silver. The flowers make small whorls of white or pink that attract bees. Thyme is equally lovely grown in pots, as an edging, or in walls and paving cracks. Thyme loves sun and any ordinary, well-drained soil. If plants become woody, chop them back by half in spring. The best types for cooking are common thyme (*Thymus vulgaris*) and lemon thyme (*Thymus* x *citriodorus*).

Marjoram

Sage

Parsley

Gold-variegated thyme

Houseplants

Some people seem to have a knack for growing houseplants well. But if you're struggling, the trick is to think of them as the plant equivalent of zoo animals – captive creatures, far from home, doing their best to survive in an alien environment. Your job is to try to mimic their natural growing conditions: the right light, heat, moisture, and food – all the little comforts of home.

A yucca grown with creeping fig (Ficus pumila) *and bird's nest fern* (Asplenium).

Some houseplants will inevitably cause problems – gardenias, for instance, are very difficult to grow well. But all the plants featured here should thrive for you.

GROWING SUCCESS

The first step is to buy plants at the peak of perfection. Look for buoyant leaves, healthy new shoots, sturdy growth, and, on flowering plants, plenty of unopened buds. Reject any with yellowed or diseased leaves, spindly growth, and, most important of all, any that have been allowed to dry out completely. If the weather's cold, insist that the plant is well wrapped for the journey home, to keep it at an even temperature.

EXPOSURE

Houseplant labels now carry much more information than they used to, so always check for the recommended exposure. In general, few plants (except for cacti) will thrive in the full blaze of afternoon sun – most prefer a spot on, or close to, a window that faces north, west, or east. In shady spots, try aspidistra, fatsia, ferns, grape ivy *(Cissus)*, and prayer plants or calatheas, but keep an eye on them and move them into a brighter location if they're not growing well. All houseplants grow towards the nearest light source, so turning them now and again will prevent them from becoming lopsided.

TEMPERATURE

Most houseplants are perfectly content at normal room temperature and don't object to your turning down the heat at night, but in very cold weather, don't leave plants trapped in the chilly gap between closed drapes and window glass. Many dislike the dry atmosphere caused by winter heating, which can cause the leaves to turn brown at the tips and margins. If this happens, you should either mist them regularly (be careful around furniture) or stand them in saucers filled with pebbles or gravel. Keep the saucers filled with water to just below the bottom of the pot, so that as the water evaporates the plants will have their own moist microclimate.

For cool bedrooms or porches, flowering houseplants such as cyclamen and calceolaria are ideal – they'll relish the conditions and flower for a much longer period. Ivies and aspidistras will also thrive here.

WATERING AND FEEDING

The frequency of watering depends on several factors – the plant, the location, the size of the pot, and the time of year, so there are no hard-and-fast rules. What you need to achieve is a balance; plants will object if they're kept dry for too long, but they'll equally turn up their noses (and often their toes) if they're given soggy conditions. It sounds confusing, but if you apply a bit of common sense you'll soon get the knack.

To check whether a plant needs watering, use the classic watering device: your finger. If the soil is dry at a depth of 1 in/2.5cm, it's time to water. Give plants a good soaking, rather than a token splash, but if there's still water in the saucer fifteen minutes later, drain it off.

Reduce watering over winter except for seasonal flowering plants, such as Christmas cactus. Houseplants are semidormant during these darker months and grow little.

Most plants can be watered from the top, but there are a few exceptions. Cyclamens grow from a saucer-shaped corm, which can collect water, and hairy-leaved plants such as African violets can trap water, which causes rotting. In all these cases, water into the saucer until the surface of the soil is moist and drain off any excess.

Houseplants should be fed every two weeks from March to September. While specific houseplant fertilizers can be used, a general one such as Schultz-Instant will suit them fine.

REPOTTING

Houseplants will outgrow their pots in time. If you suspect this is the case, check the bottom of the pot for roots emerging from the drain holes. Then knock the plant gently out of the pot and inspect the roots, to see if they're circling around the rootball. In either case, repot the plant while it's growing, in spring or early summer.

Using a houseplant or potting soil mix, put a little at the bottom of a pot that's only one or two sizes larger than the original. Put in your plant and fill in around the edges, avoiding air pockets. Firm the soil down, then water well.

Do not be tempted to just dump the plant in a very large pot and hope that it will grow even faster. Sadly, what actually happens is that the surplus soil stays soggy and stagnant after watering, causing root rots and the demise of your precious plant.

TROUBLESHOOTING

That old wives' tale about talking to your plants does make some sense, because at the same time you'll be subconsciously checking them over for dead or yellowing leaves to be removed, a little colony of aphids to be destroyed, or droopiness that indicates lack of water. All these are potential problems that you can (pardon the pun) nip in the bud.

Aphids and whitefly are the major houseplant pests. Aphids will quickly succumb to an insecticide spray such as Safer's Soap, but whitefly are more persistent. One of the most effective methods is to suck them off with a hand-held vacuum cleaner.

Scale insects are more easily overlooked, as they cling to leaves and stems tightly. They're mostly resistant to sprays, so use a suitable systemic insecticide, or remove by hand.

Red spider mites are too small to spot, but you'll see the characteristic pale leaf mottling and very fine webs. Instead of spraying, which doesn't always work, change the conditions in which the plant is growing. Red spiders love dryness, so mist the plant regularly or stand it in a water-filled saucer of gravel to increase humidity.

Mealy bugs are gray-white insects resembling tiny armadillos, often living under a disguise of white fluff. Insecticide is reasonably effective, but they can also be picked off, using a cotton swab dipped in rubbing alcohol.

Wilting is a sign of either dryness or, more often, overwatering, so check the soil mix.

Spindly growth means that you haven't been feeding enough or that the plant needs more light.

Brown crispy edges on the leaves are usually a response to hot, dry air.

Leaf drop or bud drop means that the plant has received some sort of minor shock – a change of position, a cold draft, or a period of dryness.

VACATION CARE

Most houseplants are perfectly OK without water for a week or so at average summer temperatures, as long as you water well beforehand and move them to a shady location. But for longer absences you'll need to plan.

If it's a two-week vacation, then the bathtub technique will work well. Water the plants, then line the tub with saturated newspaper or old towels. Group the plants together in the bath, where they should stay damp. If it's a sunny bathroom, give a little shade by half-closing the blinds or curtains.

For longer vacations, you could invest in some capillary matting. The plants are grouped on the matting, which constantly draws water from a reservoir as they need it. The simplest way of doing this is to set plants and matting on a draining board, placing the end of the matting into a water-filled sink. A similar system can be devised for the tub, setting the plants on upturned plastic seedtrays above the water.

Making the most of Gift plants

For Christmas and Mother's Day, garden centers are bursting with bright flowering plants – welcome gifts, but they need a little care to keep them at their best.

POINSETTIAS

Poinsettias have striking bracts. They like a warm, well-lit spot and a soil mix that's kept just moist. Most people discard them once the red or white bracts have fallen, but if you like a challenge, grow them for the following year. In late March, leave the plant unwatered for three weeks, then cut it back to 4 in/10cm and water and feed as normal through summer. To produce the colorful bracts again, keep the plant in total darkness (by covering with a black plastic bag or putting it in a closet) from 6AM to 8PM, for a period of eight weeks starting in September.

AZALEAS

Azaleas also thrive in warmth and light, but it's essential to keep the soil moist at all times. These are acid-loving plants, so if you're in a

Cyclamen persicum

Euphorbia pulcherrima *(Poinsettia)*

hard water area, use fresh rainwater or boiled (then cooled) water. In spring, after the last frosts, repot if necessary and sink the pot in a shady spot in the garden, watering and feeding regularly. Bring indoors in fall and move into a slightly larger pot using acid soil mix. With luck, you should have another fine show of flowers.

CYCLAMEN

Cyclamen are often regarded as temporary plants, but we know of one that has flourished for a staggering 54 years. The secret is to keep them as cool as possible without letting them freeze (a cool porch or greenhouse is ideal). A feeding every two weeks will prolong flowering, often for several months.

They will begin to go dormant after flowering, so gradually reduce watering until they're completely dry and store in a cool, dry place. New growth should start in summer, and you can repot them in fresh soil and begin to water again.

TEMPORARY PLANTS

Chrysanthemums and cinerarias also appreciate cool conditions, which will keep them in bloom for several weeks. They are, however, once-only plants and are best discarded after they flower.

Equally temporary are the very pretty mixed arrangements in baskets and bowls such as the one shown at left. They're crammed so full that the plants will soon exhaust the soil mix. Admire them for a few weeks, but then carefully split them up and put them into individual pots.

A gift basket is a delightful showcase for ivy and African violets.

Top Ten Houseplants

• BEGONIA

The popular flowering begonias are available year-round, but it's difficult to coax them into flower a second time. However, the 'fancy-leaved' *Begonia rex* varieties will be cheerful throughout the year. These are splendid, easy plants with striking

GROWING TIPS

Houseplants hate to be choked with dust, so clean them now and then. Glossy-leaved plants can be given a shower, then buffed with a soft tissue, while spiny plants, like cacti, and hairy plants, such as African violets, can be gently cleaned with a dust brush.

Once peat-based soil mixes have dried out completely, it's often difficult to re-wet them by conventional watering. Plunge the pots to the rim in a bowl of tepid water until thoroughly saturated, then let any surplus water drain away.

When repotting your plants you'll find that some, like African violets, have produced a number of plantlets or offsets. These can be gently pulled away from the parent plant and planted in individual small pots.

With children and pets in mind, it pays to be aware of any houseplants that can cause problems, either when touched or ingested. The only really dangerous ones are Dieffenbachia *(dumb cane) and* Brugmansia *(datura, or angel's trumpet), all parts of which are highly poisonous. Skin rashes can result from handling German primrose (*Primula obconica*) and hyacinth bulbs, although most people are unaffected.*

variegations on the large leaves. The showiest of all has a deep maroon center surrounded by stripes of pink, silver, and white-spotted green, and a purple edge. If repotted regularly, they make wonderful accent plants for a bright spot.

• CHLOROPHYTUM
(Spider plant)

With their fountains of narrow white-striped leaves and long trailing stems studded with perfectly formed plantlets, spider plants are justifiably popular. They do best in a light, airy position and should be repotted each spring to keep them at their best. They're great plants for hanging baskets and will enjoy a summer vacation in the garden, as long as you keep them well watered. Plantlets can be detached and transplanted into small pots.

• CYPERUS
(Umbrella plant)

Wonderfully architectural, with tall arching stems (to 3 ft/90cm) and a topknot of narrow leaves that spread like a many-spoked umbrella. Lovely in a light (but not sunny) window, and one of the easiest houseplants to grow – all you have to do is remember to keep it standing in water, to the rim, at all times. Just set it in an outer pot without drainage holes and keep topping it up. It's so vigorous that you'll probably have to divide it each spring (sawing through the matted roots with a large knife).

• DRACAENA

Sometimes called dragon plants, dracaenas are handsome

Spathiphyllum *(Peace lily)*

houseplants, with arching sword-shaped leaves on tall stems. Some are attractively striped, one of the finest being tricolor, with very narrow leaves edged in cream and red. Dracaenas have ambitions to be trees and will eventually shed the lower leaves to form a trunk – a mature multistemmed plant is an impressive sight. To keep them at their best, give them a warm room, a moist atmosphere, and plenty of light.

• FERNS

The Boston fern *(Nephrolepsis)* is spectacular, forming dense rosettes of deeply divided light green fronds, 2 ft/60cm and more across. They will grow in partial shade, and the key to success is to keep them well watered at all times, in a humid atmosphere – a steamy, bright bathroom suits them well. The bird's nest fern *(Asplenium)* can reach similar proportions, with the glossy undivided apple-green fronds arranged in a shuttlecock pattern; a lovely fern for a shady spot. The dainty maidenhair fern *(Adiantum)* is one of the most tempting, but you should try to resist – it is difficult to grow indoors.

✦ *FICUS BENJAMINA* (Weeping fig)

This is the finest of a large family of plants that range from the tiny creeping fig *(Ficus pumila)* to the sternly upright rubber plant *(Ficus elastica)*. The semiweeping branches and glossy leaves make this one of the most decorative of all houseplants, especially in the variegated forms. But they hate to be moved. More than likely, yours will shed a heap of leaves when you get it home; don't worry – as long as it has a warm, bright spot, free from drafts, it will quickly recover. Water regularly in summer, but it's essential to keep it on the dry side in winter.

✦ *HOWEA* (Sentry palm)

If you have a large room and a deep pocket, invest in a Sentry palm; they're very elegant. The gracefully arching stems, topped with generous fans of leaves, can reach a height of 10 ft/3m and a spread of 8 ft/2.4m. Useful, too, because they tolerate part shade and won't necessarily have to be close to a window. Set yours by a chair so that you can sit under it and dream of faraway places.

✦ *SCHEFFLERA* (Umbrella plant)

Scheffleras are bushy plants, with umbrella-like whorls of fingered glossy leaves, and can grow to more than 6 ft/1.8m. Both the plain green and the gold-variegated forms are equally tough, and this is one of the least demanding houseplants, as long as it has a reasonably bright location. If yours becomes leggy, or has ambitions to reach the ceiling, just cut it back, above a leaf joint, in spring.

✦ *SPATHIPHYLLUM* (Peace lily)

The white, hooded flowers of the peace lily are at their most plentiful in early summer, but are also produced at intervals throughout the year. Even when not in flower, it's a good looking plant, with spear-shaped glossy leaves that grow to 2 ft/60cm tall. Give it a well-lit spot and lots of moisture. This last is vital, so don't let it dry out between waterings, and place it on a water-filled saucer of gravel to keep the atmosphere humid.

✦ YUCCA

Indoor yuccas are close relatives of the popular spiky-leaved garden plants. As they grow, the lower leaves die off, until a substantial trunk has formed. If yours has outgrown its location, remove the top, repot it and keep it just moist; the chances are that it will root, as will any stem sections. Yuccas like a well-lit location, and should be allowed to dry out between waterings. Most varieties produce sharp spines at the tips of the leaves, which (for safety's sake) can be snipped off without harming the plant.

IDEAS FOR LOW-MAINTENANCE

To reduce watering, group your plants together – water evaporates from the leaves, so that a group will create its own moist microclimate. When repotting, mix water retaining crystals (from a garden center) with fresh soil mix.

Keep your glossy-leaved plants free of pore-clogging dust by giving them a shower in the kitchen sink once a month or so. Be sure to spray under the leaves as well as on top to deter red spider mites.

Epiphytes are the ultimate in low maintenance. These are jungle plants that cling to trees by their roots, taking in moisture through the leaves. Secure your plant to a piece of wood with plastic-coated wire, and mist daily with rainwater or boiled and cooled tap water, giving a very dilute liquid food every two weeks through summer.

Boston fern

Urn plant

Pineapple

Umbrella plant

Swiss cheese plant

Asparagus fern

Lawns

It's a garden paradox. While the lawn is perhaps the most unobtrusive feature of the landscape, it is also one of the most important – forming the perfect green backdrop for the rest of the garden. As professional landscapers learn early in their career, if the lawn looks good, it has a remarkable ability to make everything else look better, too.

Even if you consider it only as a play area for the kids or a place to put your garden chair, it's worth spending time to care for it.

GROWING SUCCESS
Don't try to turn it into a golf green – go for healthy and attractive instead. By selecting a grass variety right for your region and providing reasonable care, you can have a lawn to be proud of.

STARTING FROM SCRATCH
Sod or seed? Sod gives (almost) instant results but is relatively expensive and tedious to install. Seed is much cheaper, easier to use on irregularly shaped lawns, available in a wider range of grass varieties, and easier to work with. But it takes three or four months to establish and needs careful maintenance in the early stages.

PREPARING THE SOIL
Whether you decide on sod or seed, the key to a good lawn is to prepare the soil well – it may seem like an awful chore (it is), but you'll end up with a far better lawn that is unlikely to present long-term problems.

First clear the ground of any weeds or existing grass. It's particularly important to get rid of perennial weeds such as crab grass, so apply a systemic weedkiller that doesn't leave a toxic residue in the soil. Once the weeds have died back after a few weeks, they can be raked up.

Dig (or rototill) the area, incorporating plenty of organic matter such as well-rotted manure if the soil is poor. If it's really heavy, fork in lots of coarse sand or add gypsum (calcium sulfate) to improve the drainage. Rake the area level and remove any large stones, then firm it down by walking over the whole area, taking small steps

This simple, circular sweep of lawn echoes the patio design and will be relatively easy to maintain.

and rocking back on your heels (the neighbors will think you've flipped, but never mind).

Next, lightly rake the soil surface, leveling out any humps or hollows, until you're satisfied that it's flat – you can always double-check with a plank and a spirit level. Finally, rake in a starter fertilizer like 18-24-6 at 1.5 oz per sq yd/50g per sq m, a couple of days before sodding or seeding.

SOWING GRASS SEED
Early fall is the best time to sow seed – spring is fine too, but you'll have to weed and water more often while the grass is getting established.

Grass seed comes in a variety of mixes, including those for hard wear (ideal for a family lawn), for shade, and for the golf-green look. Broad-bladed grasses are used for the hardest wear, while very fine grasses are reserved for purely ornamental lawns, which need a great deal more care and attention.

The most even way to sow is to use a mechanical spreader from the garden center or tool rental. Measure out the quantity of seed needed for the area, following the package instructions to the letter – too little seed means sparse cover, too much can cause overcrowding and the possibility of disease. Use half the seed to sow the area in one direction and sow the remainder at right angles to the first, to get an even cover.

If you're sowing by hand, divide the area into sections approximately 3 ft/90cm square, using string and pegs or bamboo stakes. Weigh out the quantity needed for one section, divide it in half and put it in a plastic cup. Shake the seed level and mark this level on the inside of the cup, so that you can simply refill it rather than weighing the seed each time. Working in one section at a time, sow half the seed in one direction and the rest at right angles.

After sowing, lightly rake the seed into the soil surface and water thoroughly, using a sprinkler. Spread a light covering of straw to serve as a mulch. If birds are likely to be a problem, cover the seeded area with fine mesh plastic netting secured with stones at the edges.

Germination should start in 7-21 days, and it's important to mist the netting, in dry weather. When the grass is 1 in/2.5cm high, remove the netting and when it reaches 2 in/5cm give it a light trim back to 1 in/2.5cm. Rake up the clippings if your mower doesn't have a grass catcher and continue mowing as needed, keeping the height at 1 in/2.5cm. Once the grass is well

Newly sown or sodded lawns should be kept well watered for the first two or three months.

Individual sod pieces should be butted tightly together, and any small gaps should be filled with soil.

established, you can mow at the highest recommended height for the grass variety, never removing more than the top one-third of the grass blade.

Any weeds should be dealt with quickly before they swamp the grass seedlings. Dig out weeds carefully while they are still small or spot treat them with a low-toxicity weedkiller that will not harm the grass. And try to keep off the lawn for the first three or four months so that you don't damage the young grass.

LAYING SOD

Sod can be laid at any time of year as long as the ground isn't bone dry, waterlogged, or frozen. As with seed, however, fall and spring are best, so that you avoid dry or hot and humid weather.

Shop around to select high-quality sod that is suited to the desired use: a utility or play area can have coarser grass than an ornamental lawn. The sod should be no more than 1 in/2.5cm thick – thicker pieces are harder to establish – and be a healthy, deep green, with no bare spots or brown edges.

Sod should be laid immediately, while it's still fresh. (If this isn't possible, spread out the pieces in the shade, grass side up, and keep them well watered for a maximum of two days.) Lay the first row of sod in a straight line, butting the edges together, then stagger the joins of subsequent rows so that the finished effect resembles bricks in a wall.

Finally, trim the edges to shape. For a curved edge, use a hose or string to make the outline; for a straight edge, stretch string taut between pegs, then align a plank with it and use it as a ruler. You can use a spade to cut the edges, but a sharp knife does a neater job.

Keep the sod well watered in dry weather and don't

RENOVATING A TIRED LAWN

Even if you look after your lawn carefully, constant wear and tear takes its toll. But it's surprisingly easy to revive it.

Repair bare patches by sprinkling in 2oz per sq yd/70g per sq m of a starter fertilizer, raking it into the soil, then spreading in 1oz per sq yd/35g per sq m of grass seed. Rake the seed in, firm the surface, then cover with a thin layer of straw mulch. Water regularly in dry weather until the new grass is established.

To level humps and hollows, cut a cross through them with a spade then carefully slice under and fold back the cut sections of turf. For a hump, remove some of the soil; for a hollow, fill in the dip with extra soil. When you're satisfied that the turf is level, firm it down and water well.

If the edge of the lawn has become ragged, cut out a square of turf around the damaged section and simply turn it round, so that the lawn once again has a firm edge. Fill in the damaged section with soil and re-seed.

Overseeding – a technique often used by professionals – can totally revitalize sparse or thin grass and can be done any time during the growing season. Rake the lawn vigorously to rough up the soil surface, then spread grass seed at 1oz per sq yd/20g per sq m. Keep it well watered until the new grass is established.

Most of these jobs should be done in fall or spring, but you can work on the humps and hollows any time of year provided the ground is not frozen.

walk on it for at least a month, except to mow it. Keep it at a height of 1 in/2.5cm until the seams have joined together; then it can be mowed at the recommended height for the grass variety.

MOWING

Regular mowing creates a densely covered, healthy lawn, but never cut so low that you scalp it, producing bare patches and allowing weeds to take over.

In fact, you should err on the long side, letting the grass grow to the full recommended height for the variety – which ranges from 1 in/2.5cm for zoysia grass to 3.5 in/9cm for tall fescue. Whatever the individual height, it's important never to remove more than the top one-third of the blade. A grass with a recommended height of 2 in/5cm, for example, should be cut when it reached 3 in/7.5cm.

If your mower does not have a grass catcher, you can rake up the clippings for a neat finish. However, if the clippings are small enough or if you have used a mulching mower, which chops the clippings very fine, you can leave them right on the lawn. They will release valuable nitrogen into the soil as they decompose.

EDGING

Although it's a tedious chore, trimming the edges makes a tremendous difference to the appearance of a lawn. Long-handled shears do a neat job, but a string trimmer is easier to use. You can also install a "mowing strip" of paving, or bricks around the lawn edge, fractionally below the level of the turf, so that the mower wheels

Using a mower with a roller attachment gives a classic striped finish to a lawn.

FALL MAKE-OVER

If you want to keep your lawn looking really good, give it a full beauty treatment every second or third fall. It's extremely hard work, but both you and the lawn will be in much better shape by the time you're finished.

The first job is to remove moss and dead grass from the soil surface by raking it out. This is called "scarifying" and it can be exhausting if you're using a lawn rake. The easier alternative is to rent or buy a mechanical scarifier. You'll be surprised at the amount you rake out,

and positively shocked when you see how battle-scarred the lawn looks after you've finished – tufts and bald spots everywhere. This is perfectly normal, so don't panic.

Next, aerate to improve the drainage. For large lawns, rent a power core aerator. On small lawns you can simply use a garden fork. Insert it to a depth of 4 in/10cm and rock it back and forth, repeating at 6 in/15cm intervals. Or use inexpensive strap-on spike "shoes" to aerate the lawn.

The final step is to scatter fine compost over the whole lawn and brush it in so that it trickles into the holes you've made. This "topdressing" enriches the soil and stimulates new growth. Heavy soils will appreciate a topdressing of gypsum (calcium sulfate) to keep them open and well drained.

The fall make-over is not an essential part of lawn maintenance, but you'll be astounded at just how good your lawn looks by the following spring.

If the lawn is set lower than the surrounding paving, leave a gap between the grass and edging to minimize edge trimming.

ride over it and you can cut right to the very edge.

FEEDING

Grass is as hungry as any other plant, and a couple of applications of a slow-release lawn fertilizer works wonders, restoring even the most worn out patch. The first feeding, in spring, stimulates blade growth and greening, while a fall feeding promotes strong root growth to carry the grass through the winter. Be sure to apply the correct dosage recommended by the manufacturer and use a spreader for even coverage.

WATERING

Watering is only really necessary during a drought, assuming that a watering ban isn't in force. A healthy lawn can survive without water for a long time, but it does turn brown and is more prone to weeds afterward. If you do water, do it deeply and thoroughly. A light sprinkling is ineffective and actually makes things worse by encouraging roots to grow close to the surface. A good soaking of 1 in/2.5cm is ideal, and if you want to check this, place a jar or can marked with this measurement on the lawn

Lawn weeds can be dug out or spot treated with herbicide. For severe infestations, treat the whole lawn.

before turning on the sprinkler – once it's filled to the required level, you can turn the water off.

WEEDING

Some fertilizers are combined with weedkillers, making it easy to weed and feed at the same time. But this should only be necessary if weeds have really taken over the lawn.

Most gardeners should take a relaxed attitude toward weeds in the lawn; don't worry too much about weeds like speedwell and clover that blend in with the grasses. More thuggish weeds, such as dandelions and plantains, should be dug out or spot-treated with weedkiller.

One of the simplest ways of keeping weeds at bay is to let the grass do it for you. Let the lawn grow as high as recommended for the grass variety – up to 3 in/7.5cm for Kentucky bluegrass, for example. This not only shades out weed seedlings, but also stimulates root growth. Feeding the lawn, as well as watering during dry spells, also helps to build stronger, denser grass, which will tend to crowd out weeds, but the more you feed and water, the more often you will have to mow.

TROUBLESHOOTING

There are many lawn diseases, caused primarily by fungi. Fusarium blight (snow mold) is among the most common. It generally attacks poorly drained or overfed lawns in late winter and early spring, causing patches of turf to yellow and die and sometimes producing a fluffy white mold. You can treat it with a fungicide, but it's best controlled by improving drainage and never using a high-nitrogen fertilizer in late summer.

Moss is usually found on shaded or badly drained lawns. The instant solution is to apply a moss killer, but the beneficial effect is short-lived and will have to be re-applied every year. The long-term answer is to improve the drainage or create a beautiful moss lawn. There's little you can do about shade, but you can oversow the lawn each spring with a shade-tolerant grass mix, to revitalize it. Drainage can be improved by aerating (see Fall Make-Over).

Brown patches on the lawn in midsummer, can have numerous causes and are difficult to diagnose. Grubs consume grass roots from below, causing spongy, loose patches of turf that are easy to pull up. Control with milky spore disease or parasitic nematodes. Chinch bugs cause similar damage and are controlled with sabadilla dust.

Worm castings, on the other hand, are a good sign. A good worm population is vital to the health of the lawn, aerating it and bringing good soil to the surface. They should be encouraged, never killed.

IDEAS FOR LOW-MAINTENANCE

Minimize the amount of lawn. Use grass only in ornamental areas – to create a neutral foil for plants, for example, or an open vista – and in utility or recreation areas that will get a lot of traffic. Otherwise, install evergreen ground covers or paving.

Never plant grass on a steep slope – it will be difficult not only to get established, but also to mow and maintain. Use ground cover instead. Also don't try to grow a lawn in deep shade. In small areas, like under a tree, use an ornamental organic mulch; in larger areas, plant a shade-tolerant ground cover, like ivy. In moist, low-traffic areas, let moss take over to form a velvety carpet.

Invest in a mulching mower. This special type of power mower chops grass clippings into very fine particles that won't need to be raked up.

Low maintenance

A garden can look good year-round, yet need very little care and attention. It sounds too good to be true, doesn't it? But, with some careful planning, it's perfectly achievable; you can, honestly, spend more time relaxing in it than working in it.

There is no such thing as "no maintenance", of course – you'll always need to do some tending. But by choosing plants that virtually grow themselves, rather than picking the horticultural prima donnas, and by minimizing boring chores like lawn mowing and weeding, you'll end up saving an amazing amount of time and effort.

HOW TO CREATE A LOW-MAINTENANCE GARDEN

First of all, take a long, hard look at the design of your garden, because this can have a dramatic effect on the amount of time you spend on it. The more complicated the layout, the harder it is to maintain. Awkwardly shaped flower beds, filled with fussy plants, are pointless if you don't have the time or energy to take care of them. Could the beds be simplified? Could time-consuming small plants be replaced by a few bold, sturdy specimens? As a rule of thumb, a strong, simple design is much easier to take care of, and often looks much better.

Of course the easiest solution is to have lots of paving. But a vast expanse of uniform hardscape can look depressing. So break it up by mixing materials, like gravel and brick, and adding in plants. Lumber decking is a low-cost alternative to paving, and it's very popular with landscape designers. But it can become very slippery and dangerous in wet weather.

Self-clinging ivy and easy-care ferns are two ideal low-maintainence plants.

Next, think about your lawn. It should not take up a disproportionately large area of your yard and can readily be replaced with an evergreen ground cover. Mowing and trimming the edges of an average lawn of 120-240sq yd/100-200sq m shouldn't take more than half an hour a week. The most important thing is to keep the shape simple, avoiding wavy edges and island beds or individual plants in the lawn. Mowing a lawn containing two large flower beds can take twice as long as mowing the same-sized lawn that has no obstacles.

Edging the whole lawn with bricks or paving slabs cut out the need for edge-trimming altogether – set them just below lawn level and skim over them with the mower. And don't feed it too often – it'll only grow faster and need more cutting. Two feedings of an organic mulch a year, one in spring and the second in early fall, should be sufficient.

Your choice of plants is also important. Research carried out at a horticultural college a few years ago measured how much time is needed to care for different types of plants. On identically sized plots, a bedding scheme of annuals took 45 hours a year, a rock garden 35 hours, a mixed border 33 hours, and a shrub border 30 hours. But the shrub border underplanted with ground cover took just seven hours a year to maintain.

So it makes sense to cut back on labor-intensive plants like summer bedding and gradually introduce more easy-care shrubs. This includes the undemanding evergreen shrubs which provide the backbone of the garden, plus

Making the most of Weed beaters

Weeding is the most unpopular chore in the garden and usually the most time consuming. But weeds can be kept at bay for years if you use mulches and ground covers.

For best results, start with an all-out attack on existing weeds. Hoe out annuals such as groundsel and dig out deep-rooted perennials or use a weedkiller that contains glyphosate. Once the ground is clean, apply a 3 in/7.5cm layer of mulch. Shredded bark looks good but is relatively expensive, especially because it has to be topped up every couple of years. So use it only in the most visible areas in the garden. In less prominent areas, like the back of borders, you can use chopped leaves, ground cover corncobs, spent hops, straw, wood chips, or grass clippings. You can even use shredded newspaper.

In the long run, the most cost-effective and certainly the prettiest solution is to use ground covers to colonize the soil between shrubs and along the edges of borders. These resiliant, hard-working plants grow and spread quickly to blanket the soil and, once established, prevent most weeds from growing through. Many will also thrive in problem areas, such as steep slopes or the dry soil under trees – locations where most other plants would fail.

To get the fastest and most effective weed-smothering effect, plant the ground covers in clumps of three or more, and spread a mulch around them initially to help them get established; from then on, they'll happily require no maintenance and

A carpet of shrubs and hardy perennials suppresses weeds.

will take on the weeds themselves. Our favorites include:

Ajuga: An excellent low-growing plant, with rosettes of leaves spread on runners. Many varieties have colored foliage ('Burgundy Glow' is good), and the small spikes of blue flowers are an added attraction in spring. Grows in sun or light shade, although the cream-marked 'Variegata' is remarkably tolerant of deeper shade. It grows best in moist soils, but tolerates dry spots. Height 6 in/15cm. Plant 8 in/20cm apart.

Alchemilla (**lady's mantle**): A lovely plant that grows virtually anywhere, sun or shade, dry or damp soil. Attractive green-scalloped leaves and masses of sulphur yellow flowers carried in loose sprays. Combines beautifully with most plants and makes great flower arrangements. Height to 18 in/45cm. Plant 16 in/40cm apart.

Cotoneaster dammeri '**Coral**

Beauty': A superb evergreen forming a mound of arching stems covered in masses of tiny white flowers in late spring and coral-red berries in fall. Good in any soil, sun or part shade. Great for covering slopes. Can eventually reach a height of 3 ft/90cm and a spread of 6 ft/1.8m or more.

Geraniums: Hardy geraniums are adaptable plants and among the best for suppressing weeds. Geranium macrorrhizum has pink flowers and aromatic leaves and can take dry shade. *G. endressii* 'Wargrave Pink' grows in any good soil in sun or shade and is covered with pretty salmon-pink flowers in summer. All geraniums look wonderful as planting partners for roses. Height and planting distance is 1-2 ft/30-60cm.

Ground-cover roses: Superb in sunny sites. Varieties like 'The Fairy' and 'Mlle. Cécile Brunner' grow to around 3 ft/90cm high, flower all summer, and look lovely at the front of borders. 'William Baffin' and 'Martin Frobisher' are extremely

vigorous, spreading up to 10 ft/3m, and are ideal for hard-to-maintain banks and slopes, but don't flower quite so continuously. The new, bright pink 'Flower Carpet' is considered to be the best of all; 2^1/$_2$ ft/75cm high and 4 ft/1.2m across, it's long flowering and virtually disease free.

Lamium: One of the best for shade, where its variegated foliage really brightens up dark areas, but just as good in part sun. 'Beacon Silver' has silver-variegated leaves and clear pink flowers, but the most striking is the white-flowered 'White Nancy' which carpets the ground with fresh white-variegated foliage. Height to 6-12 in/15-30cm, spread indefinite. Plant 2 ft/60cm apart.

Nepeta (**catmint**): Besides being much loved by cats, nepeta makes a great weed suppressor. Best in a sunny spot, the gray-green foliage looks good with other plants, and the long spikes of lavender-blue flowers put on a bold display through the summer months. 'Six Hills Giant' is the toughest and tallest at 2 ft/60cm or more. Plant 1 ft/30cm apart.

Pulmonaria: These are lovely, early spring-flowering plants, easily grown in any reasonable soil but best in shade. *P. montana* 'Redstart' has soft green leaves year-round and rosy red flowers throughout spring. *P. angustifolia* 'Azurea' has bright blue flowers, while *P. officinalis* 'Sissinghurst White' produces clear white flowers followed by large white-marbled leaves. Height to 1 ft/30cm. Plant 1 ft/30cm apart.

Vinca (**periwinkle**): This glossy trailing evergreen plant, is good in full or partial shade but best in sun. It can cope with dry soil. Look for forms of *Vinca minor* – it is much more compact than the ordinary periwinkle, *Vinca major*, which is a bit invasive. 'Bowles' Variety' has lovely light blue flowers in spring and early summer and sometimes later in the year. Height 4 in/10cm. Plant 18 in/45cm apart.

plenty of weed-suppressing ground covers. You don't have to sacrifice flowers entirely, of course, but try to concentrate on a few of the long-flowering shrubs and climbers (some roses and clematis, for instance, will produce blooms right through summer) and include plenty of ground covers valued for their flowers, such as ajuga and candytuft.

Vegetables, although very rewarding to grow, are also time consuming, and fruit isn't a bowl of cherries, either. Containers and, in particular, hanging baskets provide a wonderful splash of color, but can need a great deal of watering in summer. So don't get too carried away with these labor-intensive plants – have a few, by all means, but don't overdo it.

Once you've dug up the vegetable garden and thrown out the annuals and you're looking for something more carefree to plant, make sure you stick to varieties that suit your soil, climate, and the location you want to put them in. If you don't, it'll be hard work trying to get them established, and even if they do grow, they'll be far more prone to pests and diseases. A reputable garden center should be able to advise you on the best plants for local conditions.

Hostas, rodgersias, and feathery astilbes all make ideal ground cover for a moist soil.

Top Low-Maintenance Plants

✦ TREES

A healthy well-grown tree needs absolutely minimal maintenance, but always check the mature size – trees that look small and innocent at the garden center, can grow into giants and you'll have to spend a lot of time and money keeping them

pruned back. Birch (*Betula*), hawthorn (*Crataegus*), rowan or mountain ash (*Sorbus aucuparia*), and its more upright cousin, the whitebeam (*Sorbus aria*), are mostly trouble free. The honey locust (*Gleditsia*) is tough and tolerant and grows well in dry soil – the variety 'Sunburst' is fabulous. But our favorites are the crab apples (*Malus*), beautiful spring flowers followed by long-lasting and highly decorative fruits.

✦ SHRUBS

Evergreen shrubs provide year-round structure for the garden. Many are extremely easy to grow, and among the most reliable are: winter-flowering mahonia and *Viburnum*

tinus; gold-variegated *Euonymus fortunei* 'Emerald 'n Gold' and the taller *Elaeagnus* 'Gilt Edge'; aromatic Mexican orange blossom; and, in acid soil, Japanese azaleas. Cotoneasters and barberries will also grow just about anywhere, and hollies are superb evergreen shrubs, though they're a bit slow to get established. Of the deciduous varieties, red- and yellow-stemmed dogwoods (*Cornus*) provide excellent winter color, brooms (*Cytisus*) are very free flowering in spring, and *Spiraea* 'Gold Flame' is valuable for both summer flowers and its leaf color.

✦ CLIMBERS

When buying a climber, check that it won't outgrow the space available,

The ground-covering rose 'Flower Carpet' blankets a shallow slope.

Hylotelephium *'Autumn Joy'*

to save you from constant pruning. The least trouble are the self-clinging climbers, which need no support or tying in. These include ivies (*Hedera*), climbing hydrangea (*Hydrangea petiolaris*), Virginia creeper (*Parthenocissus quinquefolia*) and Boston ivy (*Parthenocissus tricuspidata* 'Veitchii') – all of which will grow well on north walls. Twining climbers like clematis, lovely though they are, need support and regular pruning. Wall shrubs are generally well behaved, though they may need clipping to shape occasionally – pyracanthas are the toughest, but evergreen ceanothus can be wonderful in a sheltered spot.

◆ ROSES

Until recently, most roses could hardly be considered low-maintenance plants, needing a regular regimen of pruning and spraying to keep them in top shape. Thankfully, some of the newer cultivars are much easier to grow. Ground-cover roses

MINIMIZING WATERING

Using ground-cover plants, mulching, and improving the soil with bulky organic matter will all help to retain soil moisture and cut down on watering. But there will inevitably be hot, dry spells when some extra watering becomes necessary. Concentrate your efforts on the most vulnerable plants, such as those in containers and anything newly planted; established plants can tough it out in all but the severest drought. The lawn can be ignored unless it turns distressingly brown – a few thorough soakings should perk it up.

Of course, the ultimate answer for low-maintenance gardeners is to install an automatic watering system. Soaker hoses are the cheapest option and can be buried just under the soil so that water seeps out to the plants' roots. You can get a hose with tiny holes pierced along its length or a porous type that "weeps" water. Micro-drip systems are especially useful for containers, with individual sprinkler heads for each one, though

the spaghetti-like tubing has to be carefully disguised. Automatic pop-up garden sprinklers are wonderfully discreet, but much more expensive.

All these systems can be connected to battery-operated water computers that are programmed to turn the water on and off at preset times. But they are, inevitably, expensive, so it's worth getting expert advice to make sure you buy the one that's most closely tailored to your individual needs.

A drip-feed system delivers a constant trickle of water to individual plants.

are simplicity itself, needing no pruning at all, though you can shear them back almost to ground level in spring if needed. And most are remarkably disease resistant, particularly 'Flower Carpet', so spraying shouldn't be necessary. Patio roses are also worth growing, needing only a light clipping each spring.

◆ HARDY PERENNIALS

Varieties to look for are those that don't need staking or regular deadheading – two jobs that most of us could happily do without. This doesn't mean that tall varieties are out of the question – you just have to

be careful. Grasses and bamboos, for instance, can reach dizzying heights without a helping hand, and some tall herbaceous plants, like *Achillea* 'Gold Plate', have exceptional sturdy stems. All flowering perennials will have to be cut back at some stage, to remove faded stems, but with some it's a once-yearly operation. Hardy geraniums fall into this category, as do the late summer-flowering stonecrops such as 'Brilliant' and 'Autumn Joy', which provide a beautiful display of color when everything else is winding down in the fall.

Pests and diseases

There is wide range of pests and diseases that can attack the garden – some causing only annoying disfigurements and others resulting ultimately in death. But don't panic – most are opportunist, striking only when plants are stressed, and can be easily controlled or avoided.

The best way to avoid them is with good growing conditions, vigilance, and cleanliness. If you do need to resort to tougher measures, there's usually a choice of chemical or organic controls, and the new biological pest controls are a boon.

So take heart – there are many strategies to prevent pests and diseases from taking a hold and some very effective remedies if they do slip through your defenses.

PEST AND DISEASE PREVENTION

A vigorous plant is much less likely to succumb to disease or to be crippled by pest attack, so your first step is to ensure healthy soil. As we show in the chapter on soil care, however dreadful the soil you start with, you can amend it to create the fine, crumbly texture that any plant would thrive in.

GROWING HEALTHY PLANTS

When buying plants, choose the sturdiest, healthiest specimens, and reject any that show any sign of pest or disease attack. And once home, it's important to grow them in the right locations – sun-lovers like lavenders will fail in the shade and moisture-lovers like hostas will hate hot, dry places. Take care not to damage young plants, especially when planting, and keep them well watered until they become established – any check in their growth weakens them and makes them more vulnerable.

VIGILANCE

The sooner you spot a problem, the better. Most pests and diseases are very easy to deal with in the early stages, and prompt action prevents a minor irritation from becoming a full scale attack. A quick tour through

Checking plants regularly, and dealing with pests and diseases in the early stages, helps to prevent problems such as this well-established colony of aphids.

the garden at regular intervals, will let you take stock of your plants and detect any emerging problems.

CLEANLINESS

Is next to Godliness and, in a garden, next to impossible. But try to be reasonably clean and tidy. Plant debris and leaf litter are natural hiding places for slugs and snails, and diseased leaves and shoots should always be put in the trash rather than composted or left in the garden to reinfect other plants. Disinfect in a weak bleach solution any garden tools you have used on diseased plants and scrub out containers before reusing them.

Ladybugs are the natural predator of small insects, such as these aphids colonizing a bean plant.

ORGANIC CONTROLS

Organic gardeners have a number of effective techniques for dealing with pests and diseases. Foremost among them is prevention by selecting disease-resistant varieties and using sound cultural practices. If problems do occur, one good defense is physical barriers, such as simple tin-foil collars around plant stems or floating row covers to deter cutworms.

If spraying or dusting does become necessary, the chemicals used are all derived from natural sources – sulfur dust fungicide, for instance, or pyrethrum insecticide, which is made from the pyrethrum daisy. Other insecticides are based on soap – an excellent way of cleaning up the problem.

Organic gardeners cherish local wildlife as the ultimate in pest control. Birds, for instance, do a wonderful job of eating caterpillars and aphids, and frogs and toads will devour a good number of slugs. Feeders and houses for birds, ponds for frogs, and boxes for bats are all part of the organic gardener's armory.

Smaller creatures can be equally useful. Ladybugs and their larvae prey on aphids, as do the larvae of lacewings and hover flies. These predators can be attracted to the garden by providing flowers rich in nectar and pollen, such as cosmos, marguerites, yarrow, angelica, fennel, and butterfly weed. Praying mantis nymphs and adults dine on aphids, leaf hoppers, and caterpillars. Even the much-maligned wasp is beneficial: yellow jackets eat fly larvae and beetle grubs, while tiny trichogramma wasps prey on borers, gypsy moths, whiteflies, and mealybugs.

BIOLOGICAL CONTROLS

This is one of the most exciting – and effective – developments in pest control, whereby the natural enemies of a specific insect are introduced into the garden. These "enemies" might include predatory insects, parasites, or microorganisms, such as bacteria or viruses.

One such control is *Bacillus thuringiensis* (Bt), a microbial insecticide that is deadly to certain caterpillars, mosquitoes, and beetles but harmless to other insects, mammals, and the environment. Another is *Bacillus popilliae*, or milky spore disease, a bacterium that kills only Japanese beetle grubs. Parasitic nematodes are used in the lawn to control beetle grubs and in the garden to combat weevils.

Biological controls are available from mail-order sources and some garden centers.

CHEMICAL CONTROLS

These are synthetic chemical compounds and despite the current movement toward organic methods, they still have a role to play in pest and disease control, although many gardeners prefer to use them as a last resort.

Contact pesticides must come in contact with the insect to be effective, but systemic insecticides are absorbed by the plant and taken in by the insects when they feed on it. Similarly, contact fungicides act on surface fungal spores, while systemic sprays kill any trace of the disease within the plant's tissues.

Chemicals are the most instantly effective control method and the longest lasting. But they need to be used very carefully. Always follow the manufacturer's instructions to the letter, keep a separate watering can or sprayer for applying them, and store them well out of the reach of children and animals.

Pest and disease identification

This is not a comprehensive compendium of plant pests and diseases, but those listed below are the ones you're most likely to meet. If in doubt, consult your garden center; they should have a plant expert on hand who will help to identify the problem and suggest a remedy. Pests and diseases specific to individual plants (e.g, clematis wilt or lily beetle) are discussed in the relevant chapters.

Two important points:

1. When we recommend that you destroy plant material, it's vital that you do just that, by putting it in the trash. Never add it to the compost heap.

2. When using any proprietary disease treatment, whether it is organic or chemical, always check to see whether if there are any plants on which it should *not* be used. Similarly, check for any waiting period before harvesting treated fruit and vegetables.

PESTS

APHIDS

Greenfly and blackfly are the most common, but aphids come in a variety of colors, including yellow, brown, and pink. They are sap-sucking insects up to ¼in/6mm long that attack a wide variety of indoor and outdoor plants.

Aphids on a euphorbia

Symptoms: Leaves can be sticky and distorted, shoots deformed, with groups of insects clustering under the leaves and along the stems.

Prevention: Encourage ladybugs and other aphid-eating insects. Garden birds, especially chickadees, will also eat them in quantity.

Organic control: Squirt off with a jet of water or use insecticidal soap.

Biological control: There are now several aphid predators available for greenhouses. Check your local garden center.

Chemical control: Spray with insecticide. There are numerous products on the market, but it is important to look for one that doesn't harm bees, ladybugs, or lacewing larvae.

CATERPILLARS

Some caterpillars are specific to particular groups of plants such as cabbages, but others are far less discriminating and seem to eat anything in sight.

Symptoms: Leaves are eaten, usually from the edge, often giving the leaf a scalloped appearance. Plants can sometimes be stripped completely. Some caterpillars bind

Caterpillar damage to brassica leaves

leaves together with a fine silk or envelop the feeding area in a dense covering of the thread.

Prevention: Destroy eggs on the undersides of leaves. And invite birds to the garden – they'll eat the caterpillars. You can also use a barrier.

Organic control: Pick off the caterpillars by hand and squash them.

Biological control: Spray with *Bacillus thuringiensis*, a bacterium that only kills caterpillars.

Chemical control: Spray with an insecticide containing permethrin.

EARWIGS

This little brown insect, with a set of pincers at the rear, hides during the day and feeds at night on the young leaves and flowers of many plants, such as clematis, dahlias, and chrysanthemums.

Earwig

Leaf miner damage

Symptoms: Ragged holes appear in the leaves, or the edges of petals are eaten.

Prevention: Minimize their hiding places by tidying up garden debris.

Organic control: Place inverted pots, filled with straw, on stakes among the affected plants. The earwigs will hide in these and can then be destroyed.

Chemical control: Spray plants at dusk with an insecticide containing diazinon, though this is not always effective.

LEAF MINER

A surprising number of insects eat their way through the middle of leaves. Plants particularly susceptible include columbines, marguerites, lilacs, hollies, cherries, apples, and chrysanthemums.

Symptoms: Silvery-white or brown tunnels appear within the leaf. If just a few leaves are affected, this won't harm the plant.

Prevention: None.

Organic control: Pick off and destroy affected leaves.

Chemical control: Spray serious infestations with malathion.

SCALE INSECT

Indoor and greenhouse plants are most commonly affected by these sap-feeders, but many garden trees and shrubs (particularly camellias and euonymus) can be attacked.

Symptoms: Foliage is sticky with honeydew and often blackened with sooty mold. Small limpetlike scales up to ¼ in/6mm can be found on stems and the undersides of leaves.

Scale insect damage

Prevention: None.

Organic control: Pick off affected leaves if only a few have been attacked. Scale can also be washed off the leaves with soapy water.

Chemical control: Spray with malathion as soon as the problem is noticed and again in mid-to-late spring. Fruit trees can be sprayed with a horticultural oil.

SLUGS AND SNAILS

Few pests arouse quite as much passion as these do. Virtually all plants can be eaten by them and usually are. Even taller plants are not immune, since they climb to surprising heights.

Symptoms: Seedlings eaten at ground level, new shoots eaten as they appear, holes in foliage and fruit, stems stripped of leaves. Often, a silvery slime trail is visible.

Prevention: They rest in cool damp spots, so keep weeds and long grass to a minimum. Individual young plants can be protected by a circle of diatamaceous earth or grit, thorny rose cuttings or 4 in/10cm high sections of plastic bottles. You can also surround plants with copper strips.

Organic control: Various traps can be used, like half orange skins or a tuna can sunk in the ground and filled with beer (a "light" beer is best).

Night time patrols with a flashlight and bowl of salt water to sprinkle on slugs are also effective but not for the squeamish. Contact slug killers based on aluminium sulphate can be used but are expensive.

Biological control: A beneficial nematode can be watered into moist soil from spring until fall. Lasting six weeks, it doesn't kill snails but appears to give far better slug control than pellets.

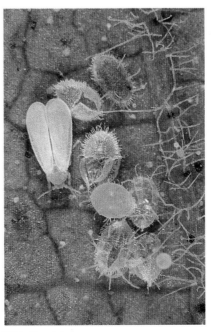
Adult vine weevil   *Vine weevil larvae in soil*

Chemical control: Scatter slug pellets thinly (4-6 in/10-15cm apart) among the plants. Replace every two weeks or so or after heavy rain. If children or pets use the garden, conceal the pellets so that they are not accidentally eaten.

....

VINE WEEVIL
Many plants, particularly cyclamen, fuchsias, impatiens, pansies, and primroses are susceptible to this rather secretive pest. The problem can be particularly bad in hanging baskets and containers.

Symptoms: Roots are eaten by a small (no more than 1 in/13mm long) white grub with a brown head, and plants slowly wilt and die. The grub later develops into a blackish, slow-moving weevil that chews irregular holes in the edges of leaves.

Prevention: Isn't easy, but as you plant newly purchased plants, check for signs of the grub in the soil.

Organic control: Remove and destroy grubs when planting. Squash adult weevils, which are most active at night.

Biological control: This is the most effective treatment. Beneficial nematodes can be watered into the soil or into pots in spring or late summer.

Chemical control: The chemicals

available to amateur growers aren't really effective.

WHITEFLY
Indoor and greenhouse plants are affected by several different types of these sap-sucking insects, and vegetables, particularly brassicas, are also susceptible.

Symptoms: Clouds of small white insects fly into the air when you brush against plants. In serious infestations, leaves are covered in sticky honeydew and a sooty mold.

Organic control: Yellow sticky traps can be hung in the greenhouse; the flies are attracted by the color and get stuck on the trap. Or you can

Whitefly with pupa cases

spray with an insecticidal soap three or four times, at five-day intervals. Also wipe leaves with cotton dipped in dilute rubbing alcohol.

Biological control: A parasitic wasp, *Encarsia formosa* (non-stinging) gives excellent control in greenhouses from mid-spring to fall.

Chemical control: Spray at least three times at five-day intervals. Unfortunately, some strains of whitefly are immune to pesticides.

PEST CONTROL TIPS

On crops such as cucumbers, zucchini, and cabbage, cover the rows with floating row covers right after seeding. Peg edges securely to keep egg-laying insects out.

Sometimes companion plants grown next to a crop or particularly susceptible plant may be able to deter pest attack. Strong smelling plants like garlic are said to deter aphids if planted next to roses, and we know from experience that pots of basil will help to keep whitefly out of the greenhouse.

An economical way to combat pests is with homemade sprays. Two spoonfuls of dish-washing soap and a drop of cooking oil mixed with 1 gallon/4 liters water makes a good insecticide against soft-bodied pests such as aphids and mites. Or mix a couple of garlic cloves or a handful of hot chili peppers with 2 cups/500 ml water in a blender; strain and spray on plants.

Use pesticides only on a calm, still day so that spray or dust does not get blown on unaffected plants or on you. And always wear protective clothing.

DISEASES
BLACKSPOT/LEAF SPOTS
Blackspot on roses is the most commonly known of the many leaf-spot diseases that can attack a wide range of plants.

Symptoms: Black or brown spots or blotches on leaves. Most are relatively harmless, but rose blackspot and spots on vegetables can be serious, so be vigilant.

Prevention: Causes too wide for generalization, but soil improvement recommended. Buy resistant rose and vegetable varieties when possible.

Organic control: Pick off and destroy affected material. Spraying with Bordeaux mixture or sulfur may help, but is not always effective.

Chemical control: There are numerous fungicides on the market to control rose blackspot and general blackspot infections.

BOTRYTIS (grey mold)
Most commonly seen on potted plants, tomatoes, cucumbers, and strawberries. The disease flourishes in damp, cool conditions and on overwatered, overcrowded, or damaged plants.

Symptoms: A fluffy grey mold followed by a slimy brown rot on leaves, stems, flowers, and fruit of soft-tissued plants.

Prevention: In the greenhouse, keep plants just moist through winter. Ensure good air circulation and do not plant too closely. In the garden, improve soil drainage.

Organic control: Remove and destroy affected parts. Once growing conditions have been improved, spraying is rarely necessary. If it is, use Bordeaux mixture.

Chemical control: Remove and destroy affected parts. Spray with a fungicide.

CLUB ROOT
Can affect all members of the cabbage (brassica) family and the closely related wallflowers and stocks.

Symptoms: Plants are stunted and roots abnormally swollen, often into "fingers." Spores can remain in the soil for many years.

Prevention: Keep soil well drained, buy resistant varieties, and do not replant brassicas in infected soil.

Organic control: Give foliar feedings with liquid seaweed.

Chemical control: Dip the plant roots/rootballs in Terraclor (PCNB) before planting time.

CORAL SPOT
Most often found on dead wood, but can spread to live wood on trees and shrubs and kill it.

Symptoms: Small, bright orange-pink pustules that are caused by a fungus.

Prevention: Clean up all infected dead wood, cut out any affected wood from trees and shrubs, and destroy it.

Organic control: None.

Chemical control: None.

DAMPING OFF
This fungus affects the roots of seedlings, especially those being revised in pots and trays. It is most common in cold, damp conditions or where seedlings are overcrowded and overwatered.

Symptoms: Collapse of seedlings and sometimes a fluffy gray fungus on the soils.

Prevention: Sow seed thinly, ensure good air circulation, don't overwater. Always use clean pots and fresh soil.

Organic control: Remove affected seedlings and the soil around their roots and improve growing conditions.

Chemical control: In severe attacks, water remaining seedlings with copper fungicide.

Grey mold on cyclamen

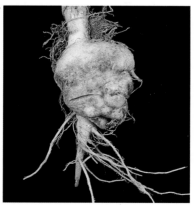

Club root on Brussels sprouts

DOWNY MILDEW

Attacks a wide range of plants and is most active during long damp spells. Can affect densely sown crops, especially in poorly drained soil.

Symptoms: A gray/white coating on the underside of leaves and a yellowing of the upper surfaces.

Prevention: Improve drainage. In greenhouses, increase ventilation and do not overwater.

Organic control: Cut out and destroy infected material. Spray remaining plants with Bordeaux mixture if attack is severe.

Chemical control: Remove affected material, then spray with a fungicide.

POWDERY MILDEW

Affects many plants and thrives in warm, dry weather – especially noticeable in fall after a hot summer. Asters, beebalm, and some roses are particularly prone.

Symptoms: A powdery white coating, usually on the upper surfaces of leaves and on fruits such as grapes and gooseberries.

Powdery mildew on rose

Prevention: Add organic matter to light or dry soils to aid moisture retention. Keep plants well watered during dry spells.

Organic control: Cut out and destroy severely affected material. Spray with an organic fungicide if attack is severe.

Chemical control: Spray with benomyl.

RUST

Affects many plants, including roses. It is spread by rain splashes and is most prevalent in humid conditions. High nitrogen in the soil, creating lush growth, seems to encourage it.

Symptoms: Orange-brown fungal spots on the leaf undersides and yellow discoloration of the surface.

Prevention: Do not overfeed plants with high-nitrogen fertilizer.

Organic control: Pick off and destroy diseased leaves. Spray susceptible plants with Bordeaux mixture early in the season.

Chemical control: As organic, but spray roses with a fungicide.

SOOTY MOLD

Sooty mold is caused by "honeydew", a sticky substance excreted by aphids, scale insects, and other sap-sucking pests that is then colonized by fungi. There is no long-term damage to the plant, but light is excluded from affected leaves, which may die. Any insect-infested plant can be affected, but plum trees seem to be especially prone.

Symptoms: A sooty black coating on leaves and stems.

Prevention: Attract birds to the garden in winter to hunt out overwintering aphids and their eggs. A dormant oil can be used on deciduous trees in winter, but follow the directions very carefully.

Organic control: On smaller trees and shrubs, use an insecticidal soap. Washing down the leaves with a stream of water helps remove the sooty deposits.

Chemical control: Spray with a systemic insecticide.

Sooty mold on a camellia

IDEAS FOR LOW-MAINTENANCE

To save time and money, choose plants that are naturally healthy and trouble free. We have tried, throughout the book, to recommend only those varieties that will need a minimum of care and attention.

Modern fruit and vegetables have been bred with a high resistance to disease, but it's always worth looking for the words "resistant to…" on a label or seed packet, to be sure.

Roses

It's no surprise that roses are the most popular flowers in the world. They offer exquisite blooms that can be as richly textured as velvet or as delicate as tissue paper, a wonderful range of colors from bright jewel tones to soft pastels, and unsurpassed fragrances.

Roses look wonderful when grown with choice companions, such as this shrub rose interplanted with violets.

It really is such a remarkable family of plants that you are bound to be captivated by one rose or another – whatever your tastes, from the romantic charms of the old-fashioned shrub roses to the bolder good looks of the modern hybrid teas and floribundas.

GROWING SUCCESS

Planting a rose is one of the wisest decisions you can make, a long-term investment that continues paying high dividends year after year.

BUYING

Take your pick from bare-root or container-grown plants. Bare-root plants are cheaper and are offered in spring or fall, usually in a protective wrapping that keeps the roots moist and should be left on until planting time. Choose those with healthy, sturdy stems and (if you can see it) a well-developed root system. Reject any with withered or brown dead stems.

Container-grown plants are available all year and are the best bet for beginning gardeners, because you're starting with a well-established root system. Again, choose one with strong shoots and also with healthy foliage that's free from pests and diseases. But check carefully that your plants are container grown, not "containerized" – that is, placed in a pot in fall and grown briefly before being sold. In effect, you're buying a bare root rose and a pot of soil, so it is a poor value. You can check by gently rocking the plant – a containerized plant will wobble.

If you're tempted by a rose standard, make sure you get your money's worth by selecting one with the straightest possible stem and a well-balanced head – reject any that are crooked or sparse.

PLANTING

Roses thrive in an open, sunny location in any reasonably fertile, well-drained soil. But it's important not to plant them in a spot recently used for rose growing. The soil there becomes "rose sick", meaning that new plants will lack vigor and never really grow well. If you have no alternative because of limited space, you'll have to dig out the old soil to 2 ft/60cm deep and wide for each rose and replace it with fresh soil from elsewhere in the garden.

The golden rule with roses is to pamper them at planting time. First water the container plant well, soak the bare-root plant in a bucket for an hour, then turn over the soil to a spade's depth, mixing in plenty of compost or well-rotted manure.

Next dig the planting hole to a depth and width that will comfortably accommodate the rootball of a container plant or the awkwardly shaped roots of a bare root – however tempting, don't economize on preparation at this stage or you'll end up with a sad, squashed plant that never does well.

Lower the plant into the hole and make sure that the knobby union of roots and stem is just at ground level. Mix the soil that you've removed with a bucketful of well-rotted manure or good compost, plus a handful of bonemeal, and fill in around the roots, firming down as you go. Water well and mulch around the plant with

more well-rotted manure or compost, to retain moisture and suppress weeds.

Climbing roses can be planted right at the base of arches, pergolas, or fences, but against a wall, where the soil is dry, try to set them at least 18 in/45cm away. They can then be trained toward the wall by planting them at a 45° angle. The various types of wall supports are discussed in the chapter on climbers, but try to ensure that there is a breathing space between the support and the wall. This allows good air circulation and helps avoid diseases such as mildew.

AFTERCARE

To encourage really vigorous growth, bush roses (hybrid teas, floribundas, and patio types) should be cut back to 3-4 in/7.5-10cm in their first spring, cutting just above outward pointing buds. Other roses can be left unpruned at this stage.

Keep the plants well watered during dry spells in their first year and feed them annually, in early spring and midsummer, with rose fertilizer. They'll do even better if you mulch them each spring with a 3 in/7.5cm layer of well-rotted manure.

Deadheading is important, too. Removing faded flowers helps encourage new shoots and a fresh supply of blooms. Ideally, cut them off a few leaves down the stem, just above an outward-facing bud.

PRUNING

Roses are pruned to keep them within bounds, promote fresh young growth, and make them produce as many flowers as possible. Except for ramblers and climbers, it's best to do the main pruning in early spring, just as the buds are beginning to break. If in doubt, err on the gentle side; you can always cut harder, after the weather settles. While pruning roses may seem mysterious, it's far easier than you might think, although the method does vary according to the type of rose. Always make clean cuts – ragged ones can cause stems to die back.

Bush roses (hybrid teas, floribundas, and miniatures) Take out any dead stems and twiggy or crossing growths, then shorten all the main stems by about one third. You should try to cut above an outward-facing bud, but don't worry too much if you can't find one. Alternatively, you just take the tops off with shearers or hedge clippers. The

MAKING THE MOST OF CLIMBERS

One of the loveliest sights in the garden is a climbing or rambling rose in full flower against a wall. They take a while to reach this impressive maturity, but you can help them along with some extra care in their first couple of years.

Regular watering and feeding are important of course, but the real secret is training. Once the shoots are long enough, bend them gently in a fan shape and train them sideways along the support – you'll find that you get many more flowers than on vertical stems. After vigorous new shoots have appeared, tie them in to the support in fall so that a good framework is established. Roses trained in this way usually flower well from top to bottom of the plant, but if yours become a little

bare-legged, take out a few of the older stems in fall to encourage new growth from the base.

If it isn't possible to train them on the horizontal (in a narrow space, for instance), choose varieties, such as 'Golden Showers' and 'Joseph's Coat', which will naturally flower well all the way up.

Climbers grown up pillars, arches, or pergolas should be trained in a spiral so that the support is evenly covered. Once the shoots reach their allotted space, just prune them back as necessary.

With their flexible stems, ramblers are easy to train in a spiral on tall poles. Seen here are 'Debutante' and 'Bleu Magenta'.

Imaginative planting

Hybrid tea and floribunda roses have traditionally been grown in formal beds, which can look effective if you use blocks of complementary colors such as lemon, gold, and white, along with a centrally placed rose standard to provide extra height. The problem with this scheme, however, is that, the roses look fine when they're in flower, dullish when they're in leaf, and downright ugly in winter. So give them a few companions to compensate. Edge the beds with low-growing evergreens such as lavender, lavender cotton (*Santolina chamaecyparissus*), or lamb's ears (*Stachys byzantina*), then tuck in a few bulbs for spring interest.

Roses mix beautifully with other shrubs and herbaceous plants in a border or a bed.

Shrub and English roses are naturals for mixed borders, especially in an informal "cottage garden" design. Their gentle colors and full, rounded flowers look perfect with foxgloves, hardy geraniums, peonies, blue or white campanulas, and the misty yellow-green flowers of lady's mantle. They're compatible with other shrubs, too, although make sure they have enough room to breathe – they hate to be confined.

All but the most vigorous roses grow well in pots, and this can be the best way to make the most of the smaller types. Miniature roses, for instance, can become overwhelmed in the general rush of garden growth and sadly overlooked. But if you put them in containers, and feed and water them regularly, they'll be only too eager to display their charms.

The simplest support can become a decorative screen or arch.

shrubs will look shocked and shorn, but it has been proved that these tools are just as effective as hand pruners… and much faster!

Shrub roses

As their name suggests, these are taller-growing roses that should be treated just like shrubs – i.e., left in peace unless they become ungainly or overgrown. Every few years, to encourage new growth, you can remove some of the oldest stems, cutting them to the base, and shorten the rest by one third.

English roses

On well-established plants, take out one or two of the oldest stems and remove any twiggy, dead, or diseased wood in spring. Cut back all other branches by about one half.

Patio, ground-cover, and miniature roses

Patio and ground-cover roses rarely need pruning. If they've outgrown their location, cut them back in spring. Miniature roses can be pruned in the same way as bush roses, or just given a trim to keep a nicely rounded shape.

Climbing and rambling roses

Climbers and ramblers take three years or so to get established and should then be pruned annually in fall. Remove any dead or damaged wood, then tip back any main shoots that have outgrown their allotted space and cut all sideshoots to 2-3 in/5-7.5cm. Some of the main stems will eventually become very woody and less productive, and these can be cut out at ground level, to encourage new shoots. Ramblers can produce new stems from the base every year, so that older stems will have to be taken out more regularly. Finally, tie in all long shoots.

Raspberry-pink 'Alexander Girault' and paler pink 'Albertine' cover a pergola.

TROUBLESHOOTING

Carefully grown roses are far less susceptible to pest and disease attacks, but even so, problems can occur. The most common pests are aphids, but you can control them with an insecticidal soap. Japanese beetles can be handpicked and destroyed or sprayed with neem, a botanical insecticide. Some varieties are particularly susceptible to the fungal diseases blackspot, mildew, and rust. These can be kept in check with a systematic fungicide.

Roses grafted onto wild rootstocks sometimes produce basal suckers, especially if you haven't planted the rose at the right depth. Suckers are usually lighter green than the true rose, with thorns of a different shape or color and sets of seven or more leaflets – so they are easy to recognize. Remove them as soon as they appear or they will sap the vigor of the plant. Dig carefully into the soil to find out where they're growing from, then snap them off. Don't cut suckers, as this only encourages them to grow more vigorously.

MAKING THE MOST OF RUGOSA ROSES

Of all the taller shrub roses, the rugosa types are the best behaved and the easiest to grow. They don't care much about soil, and diseases seem to pass them by. And they're lovely. They have small, puckered leaves; sturdy, arching stems (with a good supply of thorns); and exceptionally pretty flowers throughout summer. Just don't be put off by their names.

'Blanc Double de Coubert' is a translucent white semidouble, the flowers opening wide to give off a clean, fresh scent. 'Frau Dagmar Hastrup' is pale shell pink, single, with lovely red hips in fall. 'Roseraie de l'Haÿ' has dark, dramatic, crimson-purple double flowers with a perfume to match. Those are just three to get you started.

They're first-rate garden plants, but they will also make an excellent hedge. Plant them 4 ft/1.2m apart, keep pruning out the top growth to encourage them to be bushy, and you'll soon have a wonderful informal, semievergreen boundary to around 5 ft/1.5m tall. If you don't deadhead them, the shrubs will produce large red hips in fall.

The Top Roses

✦ HYBRID TEAS

For many, these are the classic roses – large, showy blooms, usually one to a stem, throughout summer, on upright bushes to 3 ft/90cm or so. Astonishing color range, and many are fragrant. Lots of desirable forms, and the following are especially good: **'Elina'** (a.k.a. 'Peaudouce'): pale primrose yellow – a beauty. **'Freedom'**: butter yellow, prolific flowerer. **'Just Joey'**: huge, long-lasting, copper-yellow, scented blooms. **'Royal William'**: deep velvet crimson, rich fragrance. **'Silver Jubilee'**: peachy pink, very free flowering, scented.

✦ FLORIBUNDAS

Floribundas, also flowering throughout summer, produce their flowers in clusters, giving a more colorful overall effect than hybrid teas. They're also more branched with a much looser, less formal look. Of the best and most reliable varieties, look for:

'Amber Queen': large full flowers of bright amber on neat bushes. **'Iceberg'**: white, and taller than usual at 4 ft/1.2m. Extremely long flowering. There's also a lovely climbing version. **'Korresia' (a.k.a. 'Sunsprite')**: golden yellow, fragrant, and very disease resistant. **'Sexy Rexy'**: a strange name for a lovely, clear pink flower, freely produced. **'Trumpeter'**: rich bright red, each cluster crammed with flowers.

Shrub rose 'Ballerina'

✦ SHRUB AND OLD GARDEN ROSES

Generally extremely tough, with exceptionally beautiful blooms. Take note of heights and spreads – some are quite neat, but others can be huge. Many flower only once, so in smaller gardens it's worth looking for repeat-flowerers, including: **'Ballerina'**: single pink flowers in dense clusters, very reliable. **'Buff Beauty'**: globe-shaped, scented flowers, warm apricot yellow. **'Jacqueline du Pre'**: frilly, semi-double, blush white, golden stamens, musk scent. **'White Pet'**: tiny, at 2 ft/60 cm, small white pompons, delicately scented. **'Madame Isaac Pereire'**: huge crimson flowers, very full, with magnificent scent.

✦ ENGLISH ROSES

An exciting new breed of roses raised by David Austin, combining the beauty and fragrance of the old roses with the vigor, disease resistance, and repeat flowering of modern hybrids. Most have fully double flowers and will grow to around 4 ft/1.2m, with an attractive bushy habit. We love them all, but here are a few favorites: **'Abraham Darby'**: large, cup-shaped blooms in apricot and yellow, fruity scent. **'Gertrude**

Hybrid tea 'Just Joey'

GROWING TIPS

If you've run out of wall space, climbing roses can be a lovely feature in the border, trained up a stout pole.

Roses generally need a sunny spot, but ground-cover varieties will tolerate part shade. On a north wall, try the climbers 'Golden Showers', 'New Dawn', 'Félicité et Perpétue', 'Zephirine Drouhin', and 'Gloire de Dijon'.

In addition to those varieties we've already mentioned as having good scent, the following hybrid teas are also recommended: 'Fragrant Cloud', 'Wendy Cussons', 'Papa Meilland' and 'Prima Ballerina'.

Ground-cover rose 'Kent'

English rose 'Mary Rose'

Jekyll': vibrant deep pink, strongly scented. **'Graham Thomas'**: rich yellow flowers with a strong tea-rose scent. **'Heritage'**: soft pink, cupped flowers, exceptional fragrance. **'Mary Rose'**: large, loose-petalled, pink flowers, sweetly scented – one of the most robust.

❀ PATIO ROSES

Charming dwarf versions of floribundas, most are less than 2 ft/ 60cm high – perfect for small gardens. Superb flower power for the front of borders or pots. Don't be deceived by their dainty habit – they're as tough as old boots. Look for: **'Anna Ford'**: bright orange-red, a great performer. **'Cider Cup'**: another miniature hybrid tea type, deep apricot. **'Gentle Touch'**: dainty hybrid tea-shaped flowers in pale pink. **'Sweet Dreams'**: apricot-peach and sweetly scented. **'Sweet Magic'**: orange with gold tints.

❀ GROUND-COVER ROSES

A remarkably useful group. Densely bushy, weed-smothering shrubs, some grow to only 6 in/15cm high, while others make great rambling specimens up to 6 ft/1.8m high and 15 ft/4.5m wide. Especially good for awkward spots such as steep slopes and neglected corners. Tough

and undemanding, most will flower for months on end. The best long-flowering varieties include: **'Flower Carpet'**: bright pink, 30 in/75cm high, 4 ft/1.2m spread – exceptionally disease resistant. **'Kent'**: pure white, in large clusters, 18 in/45cm high, 3 ft/90cm spread. **'Norfolk'**: fragrant double, bright yellow blooms, 18 in/45cm high, 2 ft/60cm spread. **'Surrey'**: soft pink double flowers, 2 ft/60cm high, 4 ft/1.2m spread. **'The Fairy'**: clusters of small pale pink flowers, 2 ft/60cm high, 3 ft/90cm spread.

❀ MINIATURE ROSES

Growing to no more than 18 in/ 45cm, these are tiny versions of hybrid tea and floribunda roses and

Patio rose 'Sweet Dreams'

Climbing rose 'Golden Showers'

new miniature climbers that reach only 7 ft/2.1m. The best repeat-blooming cultivars include: **'Compassion'**: apricot-pink hybrid tea flowers, sweetly scented. **'Dublin Bay'**: brilliant deep red, a sumptuous color. **'Golden Showers'**: gold, fading to cream, very free flowering. **'Good as Gold'**: miniature patio climber, clear golden yellow. **'New Dawn'**: clusters of silvery pink flowers, fruity fragrance.

❀ RAMBLING ROSES

Ramblers generally have masses of small to medium flowers in clusters and make a magnificent once-only display in early summer. They're ideal for covering large areas, and their flexible stems are easily trained on supports or can be left to ramble over an eyesore. Here are a few real gems: **'Alberic Barbier'**: creamy white, double with a fruity fragrance and virtually evergreen foliage. **'Albertine'**: large coppery pink flowers and richly scented. Vicious thorns. **'Félicité et Perpétue'**: creamy white, ruffled flowers and almost evergreen. **'Paul's Himalayan Musk'**: Pretty blush pink rosettes, up to 30 ft/9m. **'Soaring Flight'**: vigorous, disease resistant; salmon with gold-and-apricot centers.

IDEAS FOR LOW-MAINTENANCE

To minimize spraying, grow varieties that are known to be disease resistant. Trials have shown the following to be promisingly healthy: 'Flower Carpet', 'Princess Michael of Kent', 'Alexander', 'Gilda', 'Elina', 'Little Bo-Peep', 'Red Trail', and 'Telford Promise'. The climbers 'Compassion', 'Dublin Bay' and 'New Dawn' are also noted for their disease resistance.

On difficult-to-maintain slopes, try the ground-cover roses. These are vigorous carpeters that can spread up to 10 ft/3m – look for names like 'Immensee', 'Heidekönigin', 'MaxGraf', 'Pheasant', 'Red Cascade', 'Rosy Cushion', and 'Weilse Immensee'. Maintenance is easy – just lightly shear them over in spring.

are best grown in pots or in groups in the garden. Here's a selection of a small bunch: **'Angela Rippon'**: coral-pink. **'Magic Carrousel'**: white, each petal edged in red. **'Pink Symphony'**: clear pink. **'Red Ace'**: deep velvety red. **'Starina'**: bright orange-scarlet, miniature hybrid tea flowers.

❀ CLIMBING ROSES

The flowers of climbing roses are large and showy, produced singly or in small clusters, and the most desirable are those that flower again after the first summer flush. But watch for the ultimate height – some can soar to 30 ft/9m and more. Most, fortunately, are much more compact, and there are even

Miniature rose 'Starina'

Camellia x *williamsii 'Donation'*

Shrubs

If you want to minimize work in the garden, plant plenty of shrubs — compared with bedding and herbaceous plants, they're relatively care free. And they're a vital element in your garden composition, giving height and stability to what could otherwise be a boring scene in summer and a bleak one in winter.

Flowering shrubs are a delight of course, but those grown for the quality of their foliage can be just as beautiful. So cram them in, exploit the amazing range of form, color, and texture. The word 'shrub' is dull – the plants themselves are anything but.

CHOOSING

Most shrubs will grow in a wide range of soils, but a few are particular (rhododendrons and azaleas, for instance, like acid, peaty conditions). Always check what grows well and is hardy in your area – neighbors, garden centers, and the local horticultural society are all excellent sources of information.

Location can be important, too – a sun-loving rock rose (*Cistus*), for example, will fade away in the dappled shade that a mock orange (*Philadelphus*) would love. Most shrubs are pretty accommodating, falling into the "sun or partial shade" category, but if in doubt, check the label or a reference book.

At the garden center, pick out robust plants with sturdy stems and healthy leaves. Reject any that are spindly or have been in their pots for too long – a mass of weeds on the surface and lots of roots emerging from the drainage holes are the warning signs. These plants are stressed and may not adapt well when transplanted to your garden.

PLANTING AND AFTERCARE

Prepare the soil before planting by forking over the whole area and mixing in some well-rotted manure. Water the shrub, then set it in the planting hole at the same level as it was in the pot. Any roots that have wound their way around the inside of the pot should be gently teased from the rootball and carefully spread out in the planting hole to encourage them to grow sideways rather than in circles. Back fill the hole and firm down by pressing the soil around it with your foot.

Water well after planting and mulch with a layer of shredded bark, compost, or other organic matter to lock in the moisture and deter weeds. Even so, it's especially important to keep the plant well watered through any dry spells in its first year.

Afterwards give the plants a boost each spring by applying an all-purpose fertilizer such as 10-10-10 and replenishing the mulch.

Many shrubs grow well in containers and most do best in a soil mix with added slow-release fertilizer, which is fertile and well-drained. Acid-lovers such as rhododendrons can be planted in an acidic, peaty soil mix and fed with an acid-forming fertilizer.

Domes of lavender are edged with dwarf boxwood.

PRUNING

Pruning is needed to keep shrubs tidy and healthy and entails cutting out any weak, damaged, or lanky stems, and any that have become old and unproductive. But sometimes (if you didn't check the mature height and spread before planting) they need to be cut back to restrict them to their allotted space. Don't be too aggressive about it – it's dangerous to hack into a plant if you're not sure it can stand this treatment. Instead, trim them annually, so that you gradually reduce their size, by removing just a few of the older stems and pruning back the remainder by about one-third.

The best time to prune most shrubs is right after flowering (though you can delay late bloomers like Rose-of-Sharon until the spring). Pruning in the fall, while they're still growing, can encourage tender new leaves, which could be killed by frosts. Always cut back to just above a bud or pair of buds, using pruning shears that are sharp and cleaned with dilute bleach.

RENOVATING SHRUBS

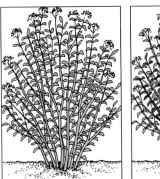

Shrubs can often become overgrown, and flowering will diminish on older stems. Prune after flowering.

To encourage new growth, cut out up to a third of the older stems to the ground, or to the main stem.

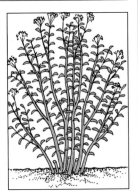

After pruning, the plant will be more open, with room for new shoots and flowers the next year.

PRUNING BUDDLEIA AND LAVATERA

These shrubs become giants unless pruned hard back every year in spring.

Cut every shoot back to within two or three pairs of buds at its base.

A fresh crop of vigorous shoots will flower later in the year.

BEST BETS FOR HEDGES

Among the most widely used hedge shrubs are yews, boxwoods, and hollies, with privet close behind. But if you're adventurous, why not pick out shrubs that will make rather more interesting, unusual boundaries.

If you want a tight-clipped hedge, *Lonicera nitida* 'Baggesen's Gold' is ideal – it's a tiny-leaved evergreen honeysuckle that's unlike the climbing forms. It grows easily from cuttings, so invest in a parent plant, stick plenty of shoots in the ground in fall, and wait for them to root. Set them out at 12 in/30cm intervals and you'll soon have a fine hedge with densely packed leaves – perfect for creating topiary if you have the time and patience.

For a less formal look, try escallonia, a pink-flowered shrub with small, glossy, evergreen leaves. Set the plants at 18 in/45cm intervals. The flowers appear in late spring, and once they fade it can be pruned to shape. Pyracantha can be treated in exactly the same way and will tolerate colder conditions than escallonia.

Lavenders make pretty flowering hedges or edgings; space the young plants 12 in/30cm apart. Remove faded flower stems in fall and rejuvenate the plants in early spring by cutting them back by half. A good variety is the compact 'Hidcote', with very deep purple-blue flowers.

SHADY CHARACTERS

Shady spots in the garden are often regarded as "difficult," but there are some remarkably decorative shrubs that will thrive.

Hydrangeas can look dry and dusty in sunny spots, but set them in dappled shade and they change character, particularly if the soil is slightly moist. They become vibrant, lush plants, the globular "mophead" flowers remaining fresh and bright for weeks.

You can almost re-create the look of a jungle if you plant *Fatsia japonica* in shade. This evergreen for mild climates makes an enormous plant,

with a mature height and spread of 10 ft/3m, and the glossy mid- green leaves can be as much as 12 in/30cm wide. Often sold as a houseplant in cold climates, it should be planted outdoors in a slightly sheltered position.

In heavier shade, lighten the gloom with two gold-variegated shrubs. The aucubas are a good choice for mild climates, and the cultivar 'Crotonifolia' has the heaviest gold patterning of all – a useful plant in any soil and situation. Equally adaptable and brighter still is another evergreen, *Elaeagnus*

pungens 'Maculata'. Each glossy, dark green leaf has a very large central splotch of bright yellow.

Elaeagnus pungens *'Maculata'*

Lovable acid-lovers

Some of the loveliest of all flowering shrubs grow best in acid, peaty soil. While many will tolerate varying degrees of lime, they'll never reach their full potential.

Rhododendrons and azaleas put on a magnificent show in early summer, the leaves almost hidden under the enormous blooms. These are all perfect plants for cool, green shade, which echoes their natural habitat and is the ideal way of displaying them. If you're planting in an open garden, set them singly – they're delightful as individual plants, but lose all their character when herded together in clashing color groups. An acidic soil is essential for rhododendrons, they'll also grow in containers filled with acid soil amended with leaf mold.

The ideal partner for the rhododendrons is pieris (Japanese andromeda), which thrives in the

same acid and slightly shaded conditions. These are handsome bushy evergreens, with bright copper-red spring growths that gradually turn green and long, dangling clusters of white lily-of-the-valley flowers. 'Forest Flame' is among the showiest.

And if you want a glossy evergreen filler plant to tone down all these bright colors, skimmia fits the bill perfectly. Densely bushy to 3 ft/ 90cm, with tiny white flowers in spring followed (on the female plants) by clusters of shiny red berries. You need to

buy male and female plants of most cultivars if you want berries, but *Skimmia reevesiana* is self-fertile.

Magnolias are less particular about soil – most of them do best in acid conditions, but some will tolerate lime as long as you dig in plenty of organic matter before planting and apply it as a generous annual mulch thereafter. These are noble plants, and one of the easiest and most popular is *M. soulangeana* – a spreading bush to 10 ft/3m, with a fine show of waxy, goblet-shaped flowers in midspring. If space is limited, choose the earlier-blooming *M. stellata*, which will take years to reach 5 ft/1.5m or so. The starry white spring flowers are sweetly scented. In cold areas, where early flowers are often hit by frost, try the slightly later-flowering *M. liliflora* 'Nigra', with purplish-pink blooms.

Rhododendron and pieris underplanted with tulips and forget-me-nots.

Top Ten Shrubs

• *BUDDLEIA DAVIDII* (Buddleia) Zones 5-9

The buddleia is adaptable and easy to grow – vigorous, hardy, and trouble-free, with long flower spikes in late summer that are a magnet for butterflies. Three of the best are 'White Profusion', lavender-blue 'Lochinch', and deep purple 'Black Knight'. Buddleias grow virtually anywhere but prefer sun and well-drained soil. Left to their own devices, they develop into enormous, ungainly bushes, so trim them back in spring to 2-3ft/60-90cm.

IDEAS FOR LOW-MAINTENANCE

Most shrubs are naturally healthy and long-lived, and a border planted entirely with shrubs is one of the easiest of all to maintain. It can be planned for year-round interest, using a good proportion of flowering and evergreen plants and exploiting contrasting leaf shapes and colors.

If you're embarking on a shrub collection, it's safest to start with those that fall into the 'virtually indestructible' category and need minimal care and attention. They include buddleia, euonymus, aucuba (laurel), forsythia, pyracantha, cotoneaster, berberis (barberry), and weigela.

Many shrubs make excellent weed-suppressing ground covers. Low growing varieties will smother weeds, while others cast a deep shade in which nothing will thrive.

• CAMELLIA Zones 7-9

Depending on the variety, camellias flower any time between November and May in mild winter climates. They prefer an acid, peaty soil but will tolerate almost any soil if given an annual mulch of acidic compost and a feeding in spring and midsummer with an acid-forming fertilizer. Frost and cold wind can damage the flower buds, so place the shrubs in a sheltered spot, facing west or north – a southern exposure is too hot, and flowers risk frost damage in an east-facing one. Keep well watered when the buds are forming toward summer and prune any straggly growths in late spring.

• *CHOISYA* (Mexican orange blossom) Zones 7-9

Deservedly popular in mild zones. Just look at its virtues – aromatic evergreen leaves; scented white flowers in late spring and also sporadically through the summer and fall; a bushy, domed shape to 6 ft/1.8m high and round; thrives in

Choisya ternata

any ordinary soil in sun or dappled shade; amazingly pest and disease free. At the northern limits of its range, it will need to be planted against a wall for shelter. The new golden form 'Sundance' is proving to be just as well-behaved as the plain green species. Choisyas need no pruning, but can be lightly trimmed back in early spring to keep them neat.

• *CORNUS* (Dogwood) Zones 2-7

The shrubby dogwoods grown for their colored stems are ideal for beds and borders. 'Elegantissima' is particularly attractive, its large leaves generously splashed with white in summer and its spiky red stems shining throughout winter. Lovely in sun or partial shade, as is the gold-variegated 'Spaethii'. 'Flavireama' has yellow stems and is a vigorous spreader. They prefer a slightly moist soil, where they'll reach a height and spread of 8 ft/ 2.4m. To stimulate bright new growth (the colors fade with age), cut a third of the stems to ground level annually in early spring.

• COTONEASTER Zones 5-8

Easy to grow and tremendously versatile. Most are evergreen, and all produce small flowers followed by long-lasting fall berries. To cover a low wall or to let tumble down a slope, try the weeping stems of 'Repens'. Any of the *C. dammeri* varieties ('Coral Beauty' is good) make excellent creeping ground cover. *Cotoneaster horizontalis* will slowly spread its fishbonelike branches against a wall, to 10 ft/3m or more. Cotoneasters grow in any soil, and while they prefer an open location, they'll tolerate north- or east-facing

Lavatera *'Barnsley'*

Spiraea *'Goldflame'*

sites so long as they're not too shady.

◆ EUONYMUS Zones 5-8

The evergreen forms of euonymus are the workhorses of the shrub border. Reliable, solid, plants that look good even in the cold weather. The lowest growing (to around 18 in/45cm) are 'Emerald 'n' Gold' and white-variegated 'Silver Queen' – though the latter starts to climb if planted near a wall. For taller plants, choose from the green-and-white 'Emerald Gaiety' (3 ft/90cm) and in zones 7-9 gold-splashed 'Aureovariegatus' (10 ft/3m). They thrive in sun or part shade in any soil and can be clipped to shape in spring. Prune out any green leaved stems on the variegated forms, as they can take over.

◆ LAVATERA (Tree mallow) Zones 6-8

A remarkable shrub that can sprint to 6 ft/1.8m high and round in a single season, with masses of hollyhock-like flowers from mid-summer to first frost. The best is the very popular 'Barnsley' – pale pink with a deeper pink eye and good for the back of a sunny border, in any well-drained soil. Cut lavateras to within 1ft/30cm of the ground in

spring (never in fall or winter, when frost could damage new growths and possibly kill the plant). 'Barnsley' sometimes sends out a branch of deeper pink flowers, and these "reversions" should be cut right back to the main stem. They're short-lived (4-5 years as a rule), and can be killed in severe winters, but they're easy to replace from semi-ripe cuttings taken in midsummer.

◆ MAHONIA Zones 4-8

Mahonias are tough and they look it, with sturdy stems and arching sprays of evergreen leathery leaves. They're stately plants (to 6-10 ft /1.8-3m) and invaluable for early spring color when the long spikes of golden flower erupt from the tip of each stem. The tender *'Charity'* is especially shapely, with delicately scented flowers, but in cold zones, opt for *Mahonia aquilifolium,* which withstands winters in zone 4. Mahonias thrive in any soil in part shade or in a sunny spot that's not too dry. If any pruning is necessary, do it in late spring. Beware of winter burn in sunny sites in cold zones.

◆ SPIREA Zones 3-8

One of the showiest summer-flowering spireas is 'Goldflame', a

GROWING TIPS

One of the prettiest shrubs for a hot, dry spot is the evergreen rock rose. The large translucent flowers, in pink or white, are produced in abundance through early and midsummer. Give them a sheltered location, and never cut back into the old wood.

Shrubs will often "layer" themselves – a branch roots where it touches the ground and forms a new plant, which can be severed from the parent and transplanted. If you want to encourage this process, bend a low-growing stem and nick it where it touches the ground (the slight wound encourages rooting). Then pin it in place with strong wire or a couple of bricks and wait. It's a good way to increase your stock of many varieties and is always worth a try.

neatly rounded shrub to 2½ ft/ 75cm. The emerging spring foliage is a soft copper-gold, maturing to variegated green gold, with fluffy rose-pink flower heads in late spring and early summer. Spireas like sun and a reasonably fertile soil. The spent flowerheads can be sheared off after flowering, and if you want to keep plants compact, cut them back to within 4 in/10cm of the ground in early spring.

◆ VIBURNUM Zones 4-8

Viburnums are easy to grow, and offer a lot of features: abundant spring flowers, handsome foliage, colorful fruits and attractive profiles. Burkwood viburnum (*Viburnum* x *burkwoodii*) grows to 10 ft/3m and bears fragrant, pink-budded, white flowers; glossy leaves; and red berries. Viburnums need moist, well-drained soil and sun or part shade.

Soil care

"A penny saved is a penny earned" goes the old saying. Turn it into garden-speak and it becomes "Take care of the soil and the plants will take care of themselves".

A mix of perennials and bedding plants thrives in well-nourished soil. A mulch of wood chips keeps down the weeds.

S oil is seen as dull old dirt that sticks to your hands and shoes and makes a mess. But if you want healthy, happy plants that shrug off pests and diseases and give you spectacular results, then the soil needs attention. So grit your teeth and read on through this chapter – out of the whole book, it's the one that's most important for successful, and easier, gardening. We won't bog you down with technical terms or complex charts, and we might throw in the odd joke, just to encourage you.

SOIL TYPES AND HOW TO IMPROVE THEM

The ideal soil is rich, dark, and crumbly. It's a kindly, receptive medium for roots, holds plant nutrients well, and is both free draining and (though it seems to be a contradiction) moisture retentive. If this is what you have in your garden, plants will grow in it like Jack's beanstalk. If you're not one of the favored few, your soil will fall into one of the following broad categories:

Clay soil is heavy and dense – when it's wet you can slice it in neat slabs; when it's dry the spade hits it with a jaw-shuddering clang and won't penetrate. The good news is that it's full of nutrients. Few plants will be able to take advantage of them, however, until you have amended it so that it is not cold and waterlogged in winter and parched in summer.

Improving a really thick clay soil takes time, but it can be done within four or five years if you keep working at it. The key is to incorporate (when digging the soil is possible) plenty of organic matter as a soil conditioner, and at the same time add coarse sand or gypsum (calcium sulfate) to aid drainage. Do this for the first couple of years and whenever you plant. In future years conditioners and amendments can be just lightly forked in – you will have encouraged worms to work the soil,

and they'll drag them down for you.

Another good way to get clay into a more crumbly state is to rough-dig it in late fall – slicing out big chunks with a spade and chopping them up. Leave them through winter, and you'll find in spring that the frost has caused all these exposed lumps to break up. You can then knock them into smaller pieces, add conditioners and amendments, and mix together.

Clay is exhausting stuff to work with, but once you have broken it down to a manageable state, it's one of the richest soils of all.

Peaty soil is dark, soft, and moisture retentive, but in its natural state it lacks the nutrients needed to grow a wide range of plants. Acid-lovers (heathers, conifers, rhododendrons, and azaleas) will enjoy this type of soil best, but once it has been improved, almost all plants will thrive in it.

Peaty soil has the invaluable quality of being both quick draining and moisture retentive – the plant remains that it is composed of trap moisture, but the air spaces in its construction prevent it from becoming waterlogged. All you have to do is add fertility. So just keep on digging in as much organic matter as your time, patience, and pocketbook will allow.

Once you've done that, and a wide variety of weeds

WORKING WITH YOUR SOIL

It is human nature to want what you can't have. If you love rhododendrons, your soil is no doubt clay, sand, or limestone instead of the acid soil they need.

You could fight back, of course, creating special acid beds for them, but the soil will eventually win and you'll find yourself tending miserable specimens that are forever ailing. That's how to turn gardening into a chore rather than a pleasure.

So work with your soil type, exploit its potential. Roses love clay – so plant them freely. Pinks (*Dianthus*) revel in the lime provided by an alkaline soil, so make a speciality of them. Sea hollies (*Eryngiums*) take on an extra luster in sandy soil, and there are many lovely forms to be explored. And of course, in an acidic soil you can plant those rhododendrons to your heart's content. To win at gardening, it's best to go with the flow.

And you needn't deprive yourself of your favorites. All garden plants, with the exception of the largest shrubs and trees, can be grown in containers, using a soil mix appropriate to the plant. It's harder work in terms of watering and feeding than growing them in open ground, but worth it for the pleasure you'll derive.

A fertile, well-drained soil that is crumbly and easy to work is the foundation for success in the garden.

start to grow, you'll know that your soil is in good shape, and you'll experience the joy of pulling out long-rooted dandelions without any resistance at all. If you detect a note of jealousy, you're a perceptive reader.

Sandy soil is one of the worst to work with. It's an inert material that acts like a sieve, with water and nutrients washing through at a rapid rate. But persistence pays dividends.

Incorporate huge amounts of organic matter, especially leaf mold and compost, to bind the sand particles and help stop the drastic loss of moisture and plant foods. But you do have to be persistent – large quantities are needed on a regular basis. Try to avoid growing plants that need regular feeding, such as roses and peonies, and don't even think about growing moisture lovers. Silver-leaved plants should do well, as will rock rose (*Cistus*), yucca, broom (*Cytisus*), yarrow, sedum, mock orange (*Philadelphus*), pinks (*Dianthus*), sea holly (*Eryngium*), crocus, and tulips. And it's ideal for growing carrots.

Limestone soil limits what you can grow. While most plants will do well in the top layer of improved soil, some of the acid-loving with vigorous root systems will start to fail when they get down to the really limy levels. The two problems you're fighting are excessive alkalinity from the chalk and the quick drainage, which creates dry conditions. There's little you can do about the former, but you can improve water-retention by digging in plenty of organic matter.

Once you have a good layer of fertile, moisture-retentive soil, most herbaceous plants and small shrubs will root into it without ever coming into contact with the limestone subsoil. Deeper-rooted trees and larger shrubs are more of a problem, so always check neighboring gardens to see what grows well. Among the better trees to try are ornamental crab apple (*Malus*), juniper, lilac, flowering cherry (*Prunus*), lilac, and yew. Useful shrubs include mock orange (*Philadelphus*), weigela, forsythia, aucuba, lilac (*Syringa*), and buddleia. One of the best climbers for an alkaline soil is honeysuckle (*Lonicera*).

Making compost

Making compost is the stuff of environmentalists' dreams – recycling kitchen and garden waste and turning it into a rich, crumbly substance that will benefit the soil (and your plants), enormously. Making your own compost is by no means obligatory, but there is something very satisfying about it.

Kitchen and household waste should yield good amounts of fruit and vegetable peelings and scraps, eggshells, coffee grounds, tea leaves, dust from the vacuum cleaner, pet hair – just about anything except meat and dairy products, which can attract visitors like rats.

The garden waste you add to the heap should be leafy or sappy material and woody prunings that have been chopped up small or shredded. Grass clippings are useful too but are best sprinkled through the heap – if you add them in bulk, they make a slimy mass. Weeds can go in (if they haven't set seed), but don't add the roots of perennials such as crab grass and dandelions, which can resprout. And never add diseased material – most diseases are very persistent and can outlive the composting process.

The neatest way of composting is to buy a ready-made bin, but you'll probably find that it's too small. You can also make a bin, using four posts and a length of 3 ft/90cm tall chicken wire. Select a site that's out of the way but convenient to the garden and exposed to sun and rain. Set the posts in the ground in a square and fasten the wire to three of the posts to make an enclosure; one side can remain open for access and be closed later with wire to a sturdy twist tie.

Lay some woody brush at the bottom of the bin to permit drainage and air circulation, then add a layer of compost material. Try to get a mix of "green" material – like grass clippings – and "brown" ones, like dead leaves. Add fresh manure or a compost activator (available from garden centers and catalogs – these nitrogen sources help the pile start "cooking" – and sprinkle a thin layer of soil over the pile every 12 in/30cm or so.

To speed decomposition, turn the pile occasionally with a garden fork, mixing the "cooler" material on the sides into the "hot" center. This keeps the pile from emitting odors. You can also poke holes in the pile with a rake handle to aid air circulation. If you're lucky, worms will move in, too, helping the compost break down even quicker.

In hot, dry weather, water the pile until it is evenly moist – like a damp sponge. In six months (in the warmer spring and summer months), you will have rich "black gold" to use in planting and as mulch.

Kitchen scraps and garden waste will eventually turn into moist, fertile, crumbly compost to enrich the soil.

Soil Conditioners

Soil conditioners are used in two ways – either dug into the soil for quick improvement or applied as a mulch around plants. Mulching suppresses weeds, retains moisture, and supplies some nutrients to the plants, and the mulching material will eventually be incorporated into the soil by worms and through decomposition.

BARK

Shredded bark makes a very attractive mulch but is rather expensive, so is best saved for "high profile" areas of the garden. Bark nuggets last up to three years before they start to break down but will eventually add fiber and nutrients. Composted bark is also available, for digging in, and has a peatlike consistency.

COCOA SHELL

Cocoa shells are a by-product of the chocolate industry and has the characteristic rich scent – an interesting fragrance for your garden. The small shells pack together into a tight mass, but they break down into the soil fairly quickly. They're slightly acid and so are useful for acid-loving plants. Their sharp edges deter slugs.

POTTING SOIL

Any of the garden center's bagged soil mixes will add bulk and fertility to the soil. This is, however, an expensive option, so use the soil mix initially for seasonal plants in containers, before spreading it in the garden.

COMPOST

Homemade compost is an excellent conditioner, both enriching and conditioning the soil at no cost at all.

LEAF MOLD

Leaf mold isn't available commercially, so you'll have to make your own. And it's so good for the garden, adding fertility and retaining moisture, that it's worth the effort. Simply gather fallen leaves into large bags each fall and store them in an out-of-the-way corner of the garden until they have rotted completely. Some towns compost leaves in fall and make the "black

GROWING TIPS

Some soil conditioners can affect the acidity of your soil. Shredded pine bark, pine needles, oak-leaf mold, chopped oak leaves, and composed sawdust from cypress or oak are all acidic and are good choices for use around azaleas, rhododendrons, pieris, and other acid-loving plants.

Even the best soil can become compacted if you walk on it in wet weather, creating a solid surface that rain can't penetrate. If this happens, fork it over lightly once it has dried.

If your soil is very infertile (if weeds struggle to grow in it, it is), organic matter will improve it in the long term. But you can give it a kick-start by adding a slow-release, all-purpose fertilizer in spring. Spread it at the manufacturer's recommended rate.

Wood chips

Cocoa shell

gold" available to residents in spring.

MANURE

Manure is one of the best all-around soil conditioners, adding both bulk and fertility to the soil. The fertility comes in the form of nitrogen, and some types are "hotter" than others: bat guano has the highest nitrogen, while cow and horse manures are a bit "colder". Nonetheless, all fresh manures can burn plants and should be composted for at least six months

Brandling worms in home-made compost

before being used around plants. Just stack it in a pile and cover it with a tarp; if needed, mix in sawdust or dead leaves to minimize any smell. You can also dig it into the soil in fall and let it cool before spring planting.

MUSHROOM SOIL

This by-product of the mushroom industry is as effective as well-rotted manure for conditioning soil. But it does contain small quantities of lime, so don't use it when planting acid-loving specimens such as rhododendrons, pieris, and azaleas.

SAND, GRIT, AND GRAVEL

Coarse sand, grit, and gravel will all improve soil immeasurably. Avoid using fine sand – it can block any air spaces and make the soil even heavier. And don't economize by using builder's sand, which contains harmful salts. You can also use the mineral gypsum (calcium sulfate) to open up really heavy clay soils.

PEAT MOSS

Peat moss was once widely used as a soil conditioner, but is falling out of favor because of concern about the effect of peat extraction on the environment. In addition, it contains very few nutrients. Save it for adding to potting soil mixes or when planting shrubs that prefer peat.

TOPSOIL

If you need large quantities of good soil in a hurry, topsoil is the answer. This is the surface layer of soil (usually removed from building sites) that is well textured and fertile. For convenience, you can buy it bagged at some garden centers, but by far the cheapest way is to have it delivered in bulk. Be sure to check it carefully before it's dumped, because the quality varies enormously and you could end up with a load of poor, stony soil or one that's full of perennial weeds.

Trees

Trees are perhaps the most important element in landscape design – they not only provide a structural framework but also contribute the dimension of height. Beyond that, they bring a range of beautiful textures and colors – with their blossoms, bark, and foliage – and add a sense of movement as their leaves stir in the wind and cast ever–changing patterns of shadows.

Trees are simply indispensable, and you will probably have a difficult time selecting just a few from the wealth of choices. There are deciduous and evergreen types, dwarfs and giants, and an astounding variety of ornamental features, including fruits, fall foliage color, growth habits, and branch structures. No matter what size yard you have, no matter what your taste or style, there is a tree that will work wonders in your garden.

GROWING SUCCESS

A tree, like a child, is for life, so do some homework before you buy.

BUYING

Check the label on the tree to make sure that it's suitable for the location you have in mind, for your soil, and for the available space.

Choose a sturdy, well-shaped tree that's obviously in good health. If it's container grown, make sure that the roots are well established but not congested or circling the rootball; ask the garden center to ease it out of the pot so you can check. Bare-root trees are a particularly good value. If possible, inspect the root system through the wrapping – it should be evenly spread, not gnarled or coiled. The most important factor with balled-and-burlapped trees – field-grown trees that have been lifted with soil around the root ball, which is wrapped in burlap – is check that the root ball hasn't been allowed to dry out.

PLANTING

Trees are planted differently than other specimens, in that the planting hole and backfill are never amended.

Silvery Pyrus salicifolia *'Pendula' (willow–leaved pear) makes a striking impact with its dense mound of weeping branches.*

Since a tree's root system eventually covers an extensive area – much larger than you could ever dig out and improve – it should adjust to the native soil when still young. If you have chosen wisely, the tree will have no problem.

Dig a hole twice as wide as but no deeper than the root ball; pierce the sides of the hole with the shovel tip. Soak bare-root trees in water for at least 24 hours; water container-grown and balled-and-burlapped types just before planting. Set the tree in the hole and remove any wire or fabric wrapping completely. Container-grown trees are set at the same depth as they were in the pot; with bare-root and balled-and-burlapped trees, the soil mark (a dark stain on the trunk) should be level with the ground. Holding the tree steady, backfill with half the soil; water in to settle the soil and let drain. Add the remaining soil and water in again.

TREES FOR IMPACT

Every tree has its own character, and some are so striking that they deserve a place as a specimen, rather than being just a background feature. Plant them as a focal point in a prominent location such as the center of a lawn.

Some trees are light and frothy, giving an airy, delicate effect. *Robinia pseudoacacia* (black locust) is one of the best of this type, especially the golden form, 'Frisia'. It grows to 30 ft/9m or more, with lots of mimosalike leaves on tiered branches. But don't plant it in an exposed spot, where strong winds can damage the brittle stems.

Equally light are birch and eucalyptus – they are lovely, open, informal trees. The trunks are colorful, too, and multi-stemmed varieties can look really stunning.

For a touch of true drama, even if it's short-lived, select a tree with spectacular blooms. The Eastern redbud (*Cercis canadensis*) explodes into a bright pink cloud in spring, while the Japanese stewartia (*Stewartia pseudocamellia*) bears delicate ivory cups in late summer.

Then there are the curiosities: Harry Lauder's walking stick (*Corylus avellana* 'Contorta'), for instance, or the corkscrew willow (*Salix babylonica* var. *pekinensis* 'Tortuosa'), which spirals to a height of 40 ft/12m – awe-inspiring when the bare branches are revealed in winter. The weeping beech (*Fagus sylvatica* 'Pendula') is outstanding too, with its drooping stems. Give it enough space, for its height of 50 ft/15m and even wider spread.

Robinia pseudoacacia *'Frisia' stands out in the middle of a lawn*

PLANTING AND STAKING A BARE-ROOT TREE

Trees are usually a good deal more expensive than shrubs or climbers and play an important role in garden design. So it pays to give them the best possible start. While the technique outlined here pertains to a bare-root tree, good ground preparation, plus careful planting and staking, is important for all types – to ensure a healthy, fast-growing tree that will give pleasure for decades.

The planting hole should be wide and deep enough to accommodate the tree roots comfortably.

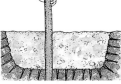

Drive in a stake (treated with a nontoxic preservative) so that 2 ft/60cm is protruding.

Set the roots over a mound of loose soil and fan them out so as to encourage them to spread.

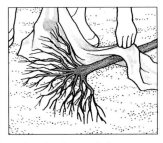

Before planting, soak the tree roots in a pail of water for 24 hours. If they are too large, wrap the roots in damp burlap.

Keeping the tree vertical, backfill the hole with soil, tamping down with your foot as you go.

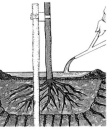

Mulch around the tree with organic matter such as compost or wood chips and soak thoroughly.

Finally, adjust the tree tie near the top of the stake so that the tree is held firmly in place.

AFTERCARE

Newly planted trees, especially bare-root trees, should be kept well watered during any dry spells in the first year. An annual feeding benefits all trees, and this can be done in late fall or in spring with an all-purpose fertilizer, such as 10-10-10. A mulch of compost or shredded bark should be spread 2-3 in/5-7.5cm thick, ideally extending out as far as the drip line.

Pruning shouldn't be necessary, except to shape the tree (by removing low-growing branches, for instance) or to take out any dead or diseased material. This is best done in late fall or winter when the tree is dormant. Trees pruned in early spring when the sap is rising can "bleed". When removing a whole branch, don't cut it flush with the trunk; cut it back to the "collar" from which it emerges, which appears as a slight swelling on the trunk.

A few trees produce suckers (new stems) around the main trunk, and these should be removed as soon as they're spotted. Snap them off as close to the point of origin as possible.

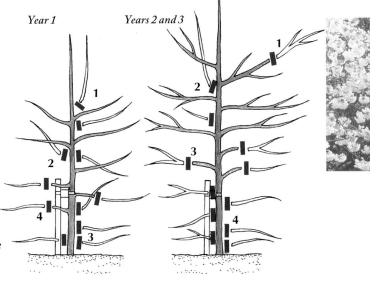

Year 1

Years 2 and 3

Formative Pruning *Year 1: Remove any competing leader shoots (1), crowded (2) or very low (3) branches, and prune back branches on the lower third of the trunk (4).*
Years 2 and 3: Continue to cut back overlong (1) or crowded (2) branches, lower branches (3) and any basal growths (4).

TREES FOR SMALL GARDENS

As stated in the introduction, there's a tree for even the smallest garden, and here are six possible candidates, all weeping varieties, just crying out for your attention:

Caragana arborescens 'Pendula' (weeping Siberian pea tree): Feathery leaves and yellow pealike flowers, to 6 ft/1.8m. Requires fertile soil in sun.

Cotoneaster salicifolius 'Pendulus' (weeping cotoneaster): A very useful grafted evergreen, to 6 ft/1.8m, with white summer flowers followed by red berries. Needs sun.

Fagus sylvatica 'Purpurea Pendula' (weeping purple beech): To 10 ft/3m, with stiffly cascading branches and very dark purple leaves. Prefers an open, sunny location.

Morus alba 'Pendula' (weeping white mulberry): A curiously gnarled and twisted tree, with long curtains of large, rough leaves, to 10 ft/3m. Needs a sunny, sheltered location

in good soil.

Salix caprea 'Pendula' (Weeping goat willow): A domed fountain of leaves to 6 ft/1.8m, with pretty spring catkins. Grows best in sun and reasonably moist soil.

Sophora japonica 'Pendula' (weeping Japanese pagoda tree): A form with a globe-shaped head of pendulous branches and leaves made up of many small leaflets. This needs a sheltered, sunny spot in fertile soil. 6 ft/1.8m.

This pea tree is ideal for a garden where space is limited.

Added-value trees

If the space available dictates that you can grow only one or two trees, it pays to shop carefully for varieties that provide more than one season of interest: spring blossoms followed by fall fruits, for instance, as with the mountain ashes (*Sorbus*) and crab apples (*Malus*). The serviceberries (*Amelanchier*) are an exceptionally good value – they are small (14 ft/4.2m), open trees, often multi-stemmed, that offer clouds of starry spring flowers, small black berries in summer, and incredibly intense fall color.

DECORATIVE BARK

If you want something that looks good year-round, select a tree with decorative bark. The shapely birches (*Betula*) become dramatic white skeletons in winter, especially if you go to the trouble of scrubbing them down. Equally striking is *Prunus serrula*, one of the small cherries,

*Serviceberry (*Amelanchier*) provides a blizzard of spring blooms.*

whose peeling mahogany-red bark is so smooth and shiny that the temptation to stroke it is irresistible. The paperbark maple (*Acer griseum*) is rough-textured, the old bark flaking to reveal the new cinnamon-colored bark beneath. The snakebark maples (*Acer capillipes, A.davidii,* and *A.pensylvanicum*) all grow to around 20 ft/6m and have beautifully patterned bark, striped with narrow vertical bands of white and green. Many members of the evergreen eucalyptus family are also attractively patterned, and one of the finest is the slender 20 ft/6m snow gum, *Eucalyptus pauciflora* ssp. *niphophila*. Silvery at first, the bark then begins to peel away in long slivers, forming a patchwork of cream, green, and gray. The snow gum is hardy to zone 8, as is the much larger *Eucalyptus gunnii*, though it tends to lean, so it's best to use a taller stake than normal to support the slender trunk for the first few years.

*One of the most decorative features of the paperbark maple (*Acer griseum*) is its peeling, colorful bark.*

Top Trees

Betula utilis '*Himalayan birch*'

native canoe or white birch (about 60 ft/18m), and European white birch (to 40 ft/12m). The latter has numerous cultivars. In smaller gardens, *Betula pendula* 'Youngii' is the one to grow, forming a wide, weeping dome to a height of around 20 ft/6m. Most birches are white stemmed, and whitest of all (dazzlingly so) is *Betula utilis* var. *jacquemontii* an upright tree to 35 ft/ 10.5m that is especially beautiful in winter.

♦ MALUS (Crab apple) Zones 3-8
The flowering crab apples are useful and decorative, especially for the small garden. Reliable and easy to grow in any soil, in sun, they put on

♦ *ACER* (Maple) Zones 2-9
This is a much-loved family of trees valued for its wonderful autumn color. Among the best small tree is the Japanese maple *Acer palmatum* 'Dissectum Atropurpureum', a shapely bronze-red mound of finely cut leaves to no more than 4 ft/1.2m (zones 5-8). Another very desirable Japanese maple is *Acer japonicum* 'Aureum', with small, golden, fan-shaped leaves, taking decades to reach 15 ft/4.5m or so (zones 5-7). All the Japanese maples need partial shade, to prevent the delicate leaves from burning in full sun.

If you have room for something taller, take a look at the snakebark and paperbark maples (see "Added-value trees" opposite), and at *Acer pseudoplatanus* 'Brilliantissimum', a round-headed tree to 20 ft/6m with typical maple leaves that emerge shrimp-pink and mature through yellow to dark green. All maples like a cool, moist (but not waterlogged) soil, and all the varieties here grow very slowly.

♦ *BETULA* (Birch) Zones 2-7
Birches have a beautiful lightness, with their open, airy habit and small, restless leaves. Tough and easy, they grow in any reasonable soil, in sun or partial shade.

Among the most popular are the

Acer pseudoplatanus '*Brilliantissimum*'

a fine show of spring blossoms followed by heavy crops of small, bright fruits. Except for 'Red Jade', they grow to around 20 ft/5m.

The orange-red fruits of 'John Downie' are the best for crab apple jelly, and it's much more upright than the rest – useful where space is tight. 'Golden Hornet' is a rounder, more spreading tree, and the heavy clusters of golden yellow fruits are spectacular in fall, persisting long

GROWING TIPS

Never plant trees too close to the house, where they can damage foundations and even (especially the thirsty willows) invade the drains. As a rule of thumb, if your house is more than 50 years old, the safe planting distance equals the eventual height of the tree. For a newer house (usually with stronger foundations), the distance can be reduced to two-thirds of the tree's mature height.

Large "specimen" trees can be extremely expensive, and although they do have instant impact, they're slower to establish than younger trees, which will take off fast and eventually catch up with them.

Inspect tree ties regularly and adjust them as necessary – a neglected tie can cut into a growing trunk and kill the tree.

Laburnums are attractive small trees, but the seeds are very poisonous. If children use the garden, plant L. × watereri 'Vossii', which sets very few seeds.

Trees are sometimes grafted onto another rootstock for added vigor or grafted as a "head" on another tree's trunk and roots. If you find alien shoots arising from just below any graft, snap them off right away or the more vigorous stock plant will take over.

after the leaves have fallen. 'Red Jade' is the baby of the family, at only 12 ft/3.6m, with a spreading, arching habit and cherry-sized, long-lasting red fruits.

◆ *PRUNUS* (Cherry) Zones 3-8

Most spring-flowering Japanese cherries are riveting when they're in bloom, but during the rest of the year, they can look pretty dull. An exception is *Prunus* 'Cheal's Weeping' (15 ft/4.5m), which has beautiful weeping habit and bronze-green leaves that turn glossy green. Another cherry with several features

to recommend it is *Prunus sargentii*, the Sargent cherry. In addition to its large, deep pink flowers, it has a graceful wide-spreading habit, attractive red-brown bark, and purplish young leaves that turn a brilliant scarlet in fall.

For striking leaf color, try black-purple *Prunus cerasifera* 'Vesuvius' It grows to a neatly rounded 25 ft/7.5m, with a good show of pink flowers in spring. Cherries thrive in any, well-drained soil in a sunny spot.

Malus 'John Downie'

❦ *SALIX* (Willow) Zones 2-7

This is a remarkable family of trees best known for the weeping types, which create long curtains of arching stems. Besides the 50 ft/15m green-stemmed Babylon weeping willow (*Salix babylonica*), there is the golden weeping willow (*Salix alba 'Tristis'*), which bears yellow branchlets and reaches 70 ft/21m.

Among the willows grown for their lovely leaves are *Salix elaeagnos*, to 45 ft/14m, which has feathery grayish foliage, and the laurel willow (*Salix pentandra*), to 60 ft/18m, which has lustrous leaves as large as those of a mountain laurel.

A smaller variety worth tracking down is the coyote willow (*Salix exigua*), a multistemmed tree to 10 ft/ 3m with long, narrow, intensely silver leaves (zones 3-6).

All willows grow fast and need plenty of water, so keep them well away from the house and any drain or sewer lines. To propagate, just root a few stems in water.

❦ *SORBUS* (Rowan, Mountain ash) Zones 3-7

These robust, undemanding plants grow in sun or partial shade in any well-drained soil and have ferny leaves, heavy clusters of fruit, and splendid fall colors. Birds devour the red-berried types, but the following are bird-proof and give a bright display.

Sorbus vilmorinii is perhaps the daintiest, at 12 ft/3.6m, with finely divided leaves on elegantly arching branches. The fruits mature from red through pink to white. *Sorbus cashmiriana* is another good choice for small gardens – a round-headed, spreading tree to 15 ft/ 4.5m, with large, shiny white

Sorbus fruits

berries. *Sorbus* x *thuringiaca* '*Fastigiata*' is much narrower, with upswept branches to around 20 ft/ 6m. The white flowers are followed by bright red fruits.

Coyote willow (Salix exigua)

IDEAS FOR LOW-MAINTENANCE

✔ *Don't plant "messy" trees – those that shed leaves, twigs, seedpods, or fruits readily – near sitting areas or paving. Cleaning up after such trees will take a lot of time, and some debris can be dangerously slippery to walk on or can stain a masonry or wood surface.*

✔ *Fertilizing large ornamental trees can be time consuming, especially when you have to portion out the correct amount of a granular fertilizer. An easy alternative is plant-food spikes, available at garden centers. Calculate the number of spikes recommended on the package for your tree's size, punch a series of holes in the soil around the tree's drip line with a stake, then slip in the spikes.*

✔ *For quick cleanup when pruning, spread a large tarp under the tree and clip away. When done, just roll it up and deposit the contents in the compost.*

Vegetables

Why bother growing your own vegetables when it's easier to buy them at the store? The simple answer is that the flavor of ultra-fresh vegetables is incomparable – and you can be sure that they have been grown organically and not sprayed with synthetic pesticides.

Another reason: if you grow from seed, you have access to all the best, latest, and more unusual varieties. And you can save money by growing vegetables like cherry tomatoes, sugar snap peas, and filet beans, that are relatively expensive to buy.

You don't even need a great deal of space for vegetables – you can grow them in pots on the patio or plant them among flowers in the border. But once you've tasted the fruits of your labors, you'll probably want a larger plot!

GROWING SUCCESS

Garden centers sell only a limited range of vegetable transplants, but if you want the best crops, growing from seed is the best option (see "Growing from Seed and Cuttings"). Free seed catalogs, advertised in newspapers and gardening magazines, are filled with information.

Select seed varieties according to your family's tastes – there's no sense growing a beautiful eggplant, for example, if no one will eat it. And take the yields into account: you may want to raise only one type of a heavy producer like zucchini.

To ensure success, choose a sunny, sheltered spot, and if the soil is poor, improve it by digging in plenty of well-rotted manure. In future years, this manure can be applied as a 3-4 in/7.5-10cm mulch in fall – the worms will do the digging for you by taking it into the soil. In pots and tubs, use a multipurpose soil mix or mix your own.

Once they're growing vigorously, it's important to keep vegetables weed free and well watered during dry spells. Keep an eye out for pests and diseases too – they shouldn't become a big problem if you deal with them immediately.

VEGETABLES IN POTS

If you have a really tiny garden, or just a balcony or a patio, you can grow vegetables in containers. Even a window box will support a mini-salad selection, with loose-leaf lettuce, green onions, radishes, cherry tomatoes, or dwarf bush beans.

Bigger vegetables need more growing room, and 12 in/30cm pots are great for eggplants, peppers, tomatoes, bush beans (4 per pot), and pole beans (2 per pot). If you want to grow zucchini, you will need a larger pot – anything up to half-barrel size. You'll get a magnificent crop.

Just as you would for any other container-grown plant, make sure the pot is free-draining and use a rich soil mix. Vegetables grow best and will produce the highest yields in a sunny spot. They will need regular watering – sometimes twice a day in hot summer weather.

As a rule, feed leafy crops, such as lettuce, with fertilizer such as 10-5-5, and fruiting crops, such as tomatoes, peppers, and zucchini, with a high-potash food like liquid tomato food or 18-18-21 after the first fruits have set.

A colorful mix of beans, parsley, and other herbs grow in pots with nasturtiums.

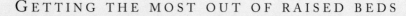

GETTING THE MOST OUT OF RAISED BEDS

This is a great way to grow vegetables, offering numerous advantages over traditional methods of vegetable gardening. Instead of being grown in widely spaced rows in a big plot, the vegetables are densely planted in a narrow bed, usually just 4 ft/1.2m wide. All the sowing, planting, weeding, and harvesting can be done from the side, without ever having to walk on the soil or bend excessively. Here are some of the benefits:

• The soil stays loose.
• The crop yield is higher than in traditional gardens because the plants are spread closer together.
• Fewer weeds because they're smothered out by densely planted crops.

• Food and water are not wasted on the spaces between rows.
• The beds are easier to manage than large plots – great for beginners, children, and busy gardeners.
• It's an ideal way of compensating for poor soil because you can build up a good fertile bed on top of it.

A raised bed should be no more than 4 ft/1.2m wide, so that you can easily reach the middle from either side, but it can be any length you like. Clear the ground of weeds and dig it over thoroughly, adding plenty of organic matter such as well-rotted manure or homemade compost. Don't walk on the soil at all after it has been dug.

Edge the bed with wooden boards, bricks, or cement blocks – this keeps

it looking neat, keeps the soil in, and hopefully, helps discourage children and pets from running through it.

Plants are set in short rows running across the bed. Because you have created high soil fertility with all the organic matter, plants are grown closer together than usual – in staggered rows that maximize the available space. When the plants are mature, they should just touch their neighbors, so that no soil is visible. Add more organic matter to the raised bed every fall, and each year the soil will become more fertile and even more productive.

If you're a beginner at vegetable gardening, start with one small bed and see how it goes. We think you'll be amazed by the results.

ORNAMENTAL GARDENS

If you don't have room for a vegetable garden, you can always grow veggies in the flower gardens. The prettier varieties, like the frilly red 'Lollo Rossa' lettuce, are remarkably attractive and will blend in well with your purely ornamental plants. To give some height to the border, grow pole beans up a tripod of bamboo canes. The scarlet flowers of 'Scarlet Runner' beans are extremely decorative, and purple-podded varieties of pole beans look positively surreal (but turn green when cooked).

At the back of the border, try artichokes, the gourmet's delight. Growing to 5 ft/1.5m, they're like magnificent giant thistles and last for many years.

Towards the front of the border, plant 'Rhubarb' Swiss chard, one of the most striking vegetables of all, with deep green spinach like leaves and bright red midribs.

Lettuces can be used as edging plants: looseleaf varieties, which don't form a dense heart, are ideal cut-and-come-again crops – just pick off a few leaves when you need them and the plants will continue to grow. Chives are good edging plants, forming dense, spiky clumps that put on a wonderful display of pink or white flowers in early summer. They'll last for years, especially if you divide them every so often.

A mix of vegetables and flowers looks delightful – and also helps to confuse insect pests.

Top Vegetables

This is our "starter-pack" choice of the easiest and most rewarding vegetables.

♦ BEANS

Pole beans and bush beans produce prolific crops in a sunny location in well-drained, fertile soil that has been liberally enriched with organic matter. The easiest way to get them started (especially if slugs are a problem in your garden) is in pots indoors, planting them out in the garden when all danger of frost has passed.

One of the prettiest (and most

GROWING TIPS

As far as possible, try to avoid growing the same type of crop in the same position every year. 'Crop rotation' helps prevent a build up of soil pests and diseases, and keeps it more fertile. The basic crop types are: brassicas (cabbages, broccoli etc), onions, peas and beans, potatoes, and root crops like carrots and turnips.

Sow fast-maturing crops to fill up space while some of the slower growing vegetables are establishing. Radishes, small lettuces, baby carrots, mini-beets and green onions are ideal. If you sow them in small batches every two weeks or so, you'll get a continuous supply rather than a glut.

Don't be too traditional about your vegetable beds – decorate with herbs, with flowers for cutting, and with strawberries.

compact) ways of growing pole beans is up a tepee of 8 ft/2.4m poles, placed 15 in/37.5cm apart in a 3 ft/90cm circle. Tie the poles together at the top or use a cane holder, and plant one bean per pole. Tie in the young shoots as they grow, keep well watered, and pinch out the leading shoot when it reaches the top of the poles. Pick regularly to encourage further cropping.

Climbing snap beans can be grown in the same way as pole beans, but the dwarf varieties should be set out in rows 10 in/25cm apart. Keep them well watered and keep picking – the pods should be tender enough to snap in half.

Troubleshooting
Protect from slugs in the early stages.

Recommended varieties
Pole beans: Kentucky Wonder, Kentucky Blue, Blue Lake FM1. Bush beans: Golden Wax, Royal Burgundy, Blue Lake 274, Tenderpod.

♦ CARROTS
Carrots need light, well-drained, fertile soil – sandy soils are perfect. Sow the seeds thinly in rows 6 in/15cm apart. For continuous cropping, sow short rows every 2-3 weeks as early as possible in spring until early summer. Thin the seedlings to 1 in/2.5cm apart and keep well watered.

Troubleshooting
The tunnelling larvae of the carrot fly are the most serious pest. The flies are attracted by the smell of the carrots, so disguise it by planting strong-scented onions or garlic nearby, and thin out seedlings in the evening when the flies are less active. They also tend to fly close to the ground, so laying down a 2-3 ft/60-90cm high barrier of plastic sheeting around the crop will keep them out. A few varieties like 'Fly Away' have some resistance to the pest.

Freshly harvested carrots

Recommended varieties

Amsterdam Forcing, Red Cored Chantenay, Fly Away, Nantes Coreless, Orlando Gold.

◆ LETTUCE

The most popular salad vegetable, and we recommend that you try some of the looseleaf varieties. They come in all shapes and colors, and the tender individual leaves can be harvested as you need them, so that you always have fresh lettuce.

Lettuce needs fertile, moisture-retentive soil and 4-6 hours of sun daily; it prefers temperatures around 65°F (18°C) and bolts in the heat. Sow outdoors at regular intervals from early spring to mid-summer, thin to 9in/23cm, and keep well watered in dry spells.

Troubleshooting

Slugs are the biggest menace. Germination can be erratic in high temperatures, so water the soil before and after sowing, to cool it down.

Recommended varieties

Butterhead: Buttercrunch, Gem.
Romaine: Apollo, Rosalita.
Looseleaf: Ruby Red, Salad Bowl.

◆ ONIONS and SHALLOTS

Incredibly easy and satisfying to grow, even if they are inexpensive in the store. Onions can be grown from seed, but it's easier to grow from sets (minibulbs) available in spring. Plant as soon as the soil is workable, 6 in/15cm apart, in a sunny, well-drained location. Push the sets in gently so that only the tips are showing and keep weeded as they grow. They're ready when the leaves

start to yellow. Shallots are grown in exactly the same way, but should be planted even earlier.

Troubleshooting

The major scourge, onion fly, only affects plants grown from seed, not from sets.

Recommended varieties

Onion: Sweet and Early, Sweet Sandwich, Walla Walla Sweet.
Shallots: Brown shallots, French shallots.

◆ PEAS

To experience the true sweetness of peas, you have to grow your own, because sugar levels begin to deteriorate just 30 minutes after picking. For maximum yields in a limited space, try the snow pea or sugar-snap types, which are eaten pod and all.

All peas need a well-drained, fertile soil. Sow them outdoors from early spring to early summer, at the planting distance recommended for the particular variety. Most peas need a little support with pea sticks, of course, but some of the semileafless varieties need little help. Water well in dry weather.

Troubleshooting

Birds love the seedlings, so cover with netting or floating row covers.

Summer squash

Recommended varieties

Shelling types: Maestro, Wando, Little Marvel.
Snow peas/sugar-snap types: Oregon Sugar Pod, Sugar Bon.

◆ POTATOES

In small gardens, early potatoes are the ones to grow – they're ready when prices are still high in the store, and they are delicious.

Seed potatoes are available from garden centers and should first be set in egg cartons on windowsills indoors and left to sprout. Plant in spring, 6 in/15cm deep, 1 ft/30cm apart, in rows 2 ft/60cm apart. As the tops grow, regularly pile up soil loosely around them. Keep well watered (essential for good crops) and start to lift them when the first flowers appear.

Troubleshooting

Potato blight is the biggest problem, especially in wet summers, but early crops are likely to escape it. Dark blotches appear on the leaves and a mold infects the tubers. Spraying with Bordeaux mixture helps, but badly affected crops should be destroyed.

Recommended varieties
Explorer, Lady Finger, Norlands, Red Pontiac.

Peas

Potatoes

✦ SQUASH

The squash family includes summer types like zucchini and yellow squash, and winter ones, such as acorn, hubbards, and butternut.

Sow seeds indoors in mid-April; buy plants at the garden center in late spring; or sow seeds directly, 3 or 4 to a hill, when the soil has warmed. Plant out when there's no longer any danger of frost, in a sunny, open spot – allow each plant a spread of 3 ft/90cm and double that for vining varieties. They can also be grown in large pots as long as they're not allowed to dry out, but they do best in a fertile soil that's had plenty of well-rotted manure added. They'll need regular watering to produce bumper crops.

For the best flavor and texture, harvest summer squash when they're no bigger than 4 in/10cm. Winter squash are harvested before the first frost, once the rinds have hardened and the vines shrivel.

Troubleshooting

The most serious pest of squash is the squash borer. The eggs hatch into white grubs and feed within the stems, causing death to the plant. Cover securely with a floating row cover at seeding or planting time for protection.

Recommended varieties

Summer squash: Aristocrat Zucchini, Early Summer crookneck, Seneca Prolific straightneck.
Winter squash: Jersey Golden Acorn, Blue Hubbard, Butterbush.

✦ TOMATOES

Tomatoes can be grown in borders, pots, and even hanging baskets. Avid gardeners grow them from seed sown indoors in early spring, but most garden centers have a good range of young plants that can be planted in a sunny, sheltered spot outdoors after the last frost. If you're lucky enough to have a greenhouse, you'll get even earlier crops.

Both bush ("determinate") and vining ("indeterminate") types need to be trained. Support them on a fence, or stake and pinch out any side shoots from the main stem, or confine them to a wire-mesh cage. Be sure to use soft cloth or soft twine. Feed lightly with a low-nitrogen food like 4-8-4 every 4-6 weeks once tiny fruits appear. Pinch out the top of the plant when four or five flower trusses have set. If you're left with lots of unripe fruit at the end of the season, just harvest the whole stem and hang it upside down in a frost-free spot to ripen.

Troubleshooting

Split or cracked skin, or a brown rot at the base of the fruit (blossom-end rot), is caused by irregular watering.

IDEAS FOR LOW-MAINTENANCE

Weeding is one of the most time consuming tasks. An easy way to minimize it with crops like potatoes, zucchini, and tomatoes, is to grow them through black plastic mulch, which stops the weeds completely. Lay it over the planting area, bury the edges, and plant through cross-shaped slits. Tuck a few slug pellets under the plastic to keep these pests at bay.

To minimize time spent watering, use a soaker hose. This can be laid along the rows or buried 4 in/10cm deep before planting and will wet a 18in/45cm band of soil around the plants. It is far more efficient than using a sprinkler.

Some varieties of vegetables have been specially bred to resist pests and diseases. Growing them will result in a healthier garden and mean less work.

Recommended varieties

Bush: Celebrity VFNT, Tumbler.
Vining: Beefsteak, Better Boy, Early.
Cherry: Super Sweet 100.

Ripening tomatoes

Water gardening

Water in the garden is like a magnet – whether a clear, still reflecting pool or an effervescent fountain dancing in the sun, it attracts our attention and draws us in. A water feature provides soothing music for our ears, is refreshing to the touch, and adds a dramatic visual element that can be richly planted or left elegantly unadorned.

Iris laevigata

They're mostly low maintenance, too. Plants will need to be divided every few years, and a thorough dredging operation may be necessary at some point, but otherwise there's very little work involved. The most time-consuming aspect of water gardening is sitting back and enjoying it.

HOW TO CREATE A GARDEN POND
LOCATION

A sunny location is best if you want to grow sun-loving plants like water lilies. But you can perk up a shady site with a water garden, and most plants, especially grasses and sedges, will grow well. However, try to avoid the shade cast by trees – fallen leaves pollute the water, harming plant and animal life, and will need to be cleaned up regularly. Also make sure the site's level, too, or the water will look like it's going to spill out.

CONSTRUCTION

Preformed plastic or fiberglass pools seem like an "instant" solution, but they can be tricky to install unless the shape is very simple. Using a flexible butyl rubber or PVC liner gives you much more freedom to create a pond that fits your site and suits the garden design. Always use a good-quality liner (look for a 20-year guarantee), unless you want to go through the headache of constantly draining and patching a leaking pond.

Mark out the pond shape using garden hose for a curved pond or stakes and string for a square or rectangle. To calculate the size of liner you'll need, use the following equation:

Length = overall length of pool + twice maximum depth
Width = overall width of pool + twice maximum depth

Dig out the area so that you create a series of 10 in/ 25cm shelves stepped down from the edge – water plants vary in the depth of water they need, and this will allow you to plant a wide selection.

To let birds take a bath and give frogs an easy exit route, make at least one "beach" area that slopes very gently from the edge. At the center of the excavation, try to achieve a depth of at least 2 ft/60cm; this will help keep the area unfrozen through cold winter weather and will help protect fish and pond life.

Once the digging is done, remove any sharp stones or debris that could puncture the liner. As an extra precaution, you can line the hole with sand or with sheets of fiberglass insulation or landscape fabric. Drape the liner centrally over the hole, weigh down the edges, then fill from a hose – you'll find that the liner molds to the shape of the hole simply by the weight of the water.

The gentle murmur of running water adds an extra dimension to this tranquil pool.

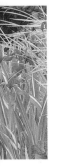

CHILDPROOF WATER

Even shallow ponds can be a hazard to children, but that doesn't mean you can't have water in the garden. There are ready-made features galore, from wall fountains to water-bathed millstones, but one of the simplest is a bubble pool, which you can put together in an afternoon once you have purchased:

- 1 low-voltage pond pump with extension pipe
- 1 waterproof tank (e.g. water heater tank)
- 1 square of rigid mesh
- Pebbles or attractive stones

Sink the tank, fill with water, install the pump, and position the extension pipe so that it is 3–4 in/7.5–10cm above ground level. Place mesh over the tank and mound up the stones to disguise it. Switch on. Water will bubble and gurgle from the pipe and splash over the stones back into the tank. Frogs and birds will love it too.

CAUTION: Water and electricity can be a lethal combination, so always use a ground fault circuit interrupter. And protect any ground-level cable by threading it through rigid metal or plastic tubing, to avoid the possibility of accidentally slicing through it while gardening.

A sparkling water feature such as this one in a tub can be tucked into even the smallest garden and surrounded by moisture-loving plants.

Once the pond is full, trim off the excess liner, leaving an overlap of around 6 in/15cm. This is best disguised by a surround of decorative rocks or paving slabs that overhangs the pond slightly; in a lawn you can simply tuck the edge under the turf. Finally, leave the water for a week or so before doing any planting or stocking with fish, to allow any tap-water additives to disperse.

PLANTING

Water-garden centers stock an excellent range of plants. But if there isn't one near you, there are several very good mail-order sources who advertise in gardening magazines.

Oxygenating plants such as elodea are essential. They produce most of their growth underwater, helping to suppress algae and supply oxygen for fish and for the general health of the water. They're sold in bunches, so allow four or five bunches for every square yard or meter.

These oxygenators, plus bare-root water lilies, and plants in very small pots, will need to be placed in plastic-mesh planting baskets. As a guide, a 12 in/30cm basket will accommodate 12 oxygenating plants or one water lily.

Line the basket with burlap unless the mesh is very fine and fill with aquatic soil mix or garden soil – heavy soil that's not too fertile is ideal. Settle the plants so that the point from which the top growth emerges is just at soil level. Top with a 1 in/13mm layer of gravel or small stones, to stop the soil from washing away.

Set the basket in the pond at the recommended planting depth (the distance between the top of the pot and the surface of the water), adjusting the height with bricks if necessary. Young lilies can be set high initially, so that the leaves are on the surface, and gradually lowered to the right depth as the leaves lengthen.

AFTERCARE

Keep the water as clean as possible by regularly removing any fallen leaves and clear away all dead top growth in fall, along with a good proportion of the oxygenating plants if they have become congested.

In winter, toxic gases harmful to fish can build up if the pond is frozen for several days. Never smash the ice to break it (the shock waves could kill the fish) – just set a

pan of boiling water on the surface until it has melted. You can also install a pond heater – it's cheap to run and relatively cheap to buy.

Plants will eventually outgrow their baskets and should be lifted and divided in spring or summer (taking care to hose off any water creatures such as pollywogs as you lift). Some roots are easy to tease apart, but others are so dense that you may have to cut them with a knife or saw. Replant the best portions in fresh soil mix.

If debris has built up in the bottom of the pond, refresh the water by siphoning off half the volume and refilling from a trickling hose. If the buildup is severe, then drain the pond and clean it out – a tedious task that will make you wish you'd cleaned the debris out regularly. If the pond is a haven for wildlife, leave the bottom couple of inches of mud, which harbors all kinds of animals, and do the cleaning in fall – in spring, you might disrupt spawning frogs or emerging pollywogs.

TROUBLESHOOTING

Ponds are generally very little trouble. It's normal for a new pond to develop a pea-soup look, due to algae. But this can be discouraged by using plenty of oxygenating plants, adding water snails to keep down debris, and planting water lilies to provide shade. **Blanketweed** is a spreading form of algae, with long green filaments. It can be raked out or easily twirled around a stick, as if making cotton candy. The tiny floating plants known as duckweed look pretty in small numbers, but they soon spread – scoop them off the surface of the water with a net. Aphids are easily disposed of by squirting them with a jet from the hose.

Candelabra primulas and Iris ensata *love the boggy conditions at pool edges.*

MAKING THE MOST OF WATER LILIES

Water lilies (*Nymphaea*) are a must for any pond or pool in a sunny spot. The flowers are beautiful and the leaves are both decorative and useful – they shade the water, keeping down the algae growth that flourishes in sun. They also provide a cool hiding place for fish and a launching pad for frogs. Tropical water lilies are suitable only for zones 9-10 or can be grown as annuals. Hardy types will overwinter in most climates; ask the supplier or read the label for zone information. Those listed here are all hardy.

Before you grab the first plant that catches your eye, check the eventual spread, in case it's more suited to a vast lake than a domestic pool. The

Beautiful and useful water lilies.

aim is to find a plant that will take up around one-third of the pool, creating a nice balance of leaf and open water.

In very small ponds, or in water barrels, the dwarf 'Helvola' is a little yellow gem, spreading to only 16 in/40cm or so. Also compact is the yellow to orange 'Paul Hariot'. Both should be planted 6-9 in/15-23cm deep.

The Laydekeri hybrids are wider, at up to 3 ft/90cm, and Leydekeri 'Purpurata' is a good one. Plant it 9 in/23cm deep.

The rose-crimson 'James Brydon', at 4 ft/1.2m, is a reliable old favorite, but for more substantial stretches of water, look for the Marliacea hybrids. Some of these will spread to 6 ft/18m at a planting depth of 12 in/30cm or more. The white 'Marliac Albida' is exceptionally free-flowering and fragrant.

And if your pond is really more like a lake, water lilies like yellow 'Colonel A. J. Welch' and deep pink 'Charles de Meurville', at 8 ft/2.4m wide, planted 2 ft/60cm deep, will fill it beautifully.

Top Ten Water Plants

Aponogeton distachyos

Caltha palustris

Mimulus luteus

◆ *APONOGETON DISTACHYOS*
(Cape pond weed) Zones 9-10

These are extraordinary white flowers with black stamens and a vanilla scent. They're produced on short spikes at almost any time of year, but the two main flushes are in late spring and fall. The long, strap-shaped leaves float on the water in the same way as water lilies do. Young plants should be set at a depth

GROWING TIPS

Fish bring life and color to a pond, but are inadvisable if you're especially interested in wildlife; they feed voraciously on pollywogs, baby frogs and other small pond creatures.

Algae can form on the paved or timber edges of ponds, making them dangerously slippery. Clean them down using a scrubbing brush and dilute dish washing liquid; never use chemical path cleaners which could leach into the water and harm plants and pond life.

Ramshorns are the most useful pond snails – they clear up debris and never snack on pond plants.

of 6 in/15cm, but once established, they can gradually be lowered to as deep as 18 in/45cm. Needs full sun.

◆ *CALTHA PALUSTRIS*
(Marsh marigold) Zones 3-8

A lovely pond-edge plant, with mounds of shiny, heart-shaped, dark green leaves that are covered with giant "buttercups" in spring. The showiest of all is 'Multiplex', a very full-petalled double form that sometimes flowers again later in the year. Plant in the shallow end, at a depth of no more than 2 in/5cm.

Japanese Iris

◆ *CAREX ELATA* 'AUREA'
(Bowles' golden sedge) Zones 6-9

One of the brightest sedges, and one of the least invasive, forming a neatly rounded clump of gold to a height of 12 in/30cm. Plant 1 in/2.5cm deep or in boggy soil at the edge of the pond.

◆ *CYPERUS ERAGROSTIS*
(Umbrella grass) Zones 8-10

A close relation of the indoor umbrella plant, with the same arching stems and leafy topknots, that grow to a height of 2 ft/60cm. Plant at any depth up to 6 in/15cm. It's also sold as *Cyperus vegetus* and is preferable to *Cyperus longus*, which can be extremely invasive.

◆ IRIS (Zones 4-8)

Grow them for their beauty, ignoring the fact that the flowering period is only a few weeks. There's a vast range: from *Iris ensata* (sometimes sold as *Iris kaempferi*), which grows in only 1 in/2.5cm of water or in boggy soil; through *Iris laevigata* at 2-3 in/5-7.5cm deep; to *Iris pseudacorus*, which is best suited to large ponds, at a depth of up to 18 in/45cm. When you're shopping for *I. ensata*, look for the Higo hybrids, which have exceptionally large, showy flowers.

◆ *MIMULUS LUTEUS* (Yellow monkey flower) Zones 6-8

Cheerful yellow flowers produced all summer long. They can be grown as a pool side plant in boggy soil, but are hardiest when planted in water at a depth of 3 in/7.5cm. Annual forms of monkey flower sold as bedding plants, will grow in shallow water.

◆ *MYOSOTIS SCORPIOIDES* (Water forget-me-not) Zones 5-8

A haze of bright blue flowers from late spring to summer to 12 in/30cm or so. Midblue 'Sapphire' is especially attractive. Plant in soggy soil at the pond edge, or up to 3 in/7.5cm deep in the water. Not reliably long-lived, but seedlings should be plentiful.

◆ *NYMPHAEA* (Water lily) Zones 4-10

The essential water plant for a sunny spot. But very expensive, so take care when buying and planting. Water lilies vary tremendously in spread, with some suitable for a water barrel and others for an ornamental lake. But they like a peaceful life, in still water, so don't plant them near a fountain or any other moving water feature.

◆ *TYPHA MINIMA* (Dwarf cattail) Zones 6-9

A delightful small cattail that won't take over the whole pond. Grows to 18 in/45cm in 2-6 in/5-15cm of water. Great for cutting – spray the seedheads with hair spray to "fix" them.

Myosotis scorpioides

Zantedeschia aethiopica

◆ *ZANTEDESCHIA AETHIOPICA* (Calla lily) Zones 7-10

Stately white flowers to 3 ft/90 cm from March to June and handsome arrow-shaped foliage. It has a reputation for being tender, but the secret is to plant it deep – 6 in/15cm is about right. 'Crowborough' is one of the hardiest once established. There are also lovely dwarf forms.

IDEAS FOR LOW-MAINTENANCE

Place a fine mesh net over the pond in fall, to catch falling leaves – much easier than fishing them out on a daily basis.

When buying plants, steer clear of any described as 'vigorous'; the likelihood is that they will be horribly invasive and need severe cutting back every year.

Unplanted, unstocked pools can be very pleasing – a simple circle of water, for instance, surrounded by attractive paving, makes a lovely feature. In a shady spot, give it extra sparkle by installing a fountain.

Weed control

Weeds are opportunists, taking advantage of any gap in our defenses – popping up from underground stems, floating in on air-borne seeds, even attaching their seedheads to our clothes and hitching a ride. They are experts in the art of invasion.

Chickweed

They look sloppy, they steal water and nutrients, they can smother precious plants, and they're a nuisance. But once you've dealt with the most invasive types and the garden is fully planted, you'll find that the time spent weeding is reduced to the few seconds it takes to pull out the occasional interloper.

CONTROL METHODS

Hand weeding: Pulling weeds by hand or prying them out with a trowel is a good way of getting rid of shallow-rooted weeds and is easiest when the ground is moist.

Hoeing: This is by far the quickest way of eliminating weed seedlings. Draw hoes have curved necks and downward-facing blades that are good for chopping weeds. Dutch scuffle or push-hoes have a forward facing blade that is pushed just under the weeds at root level. If the soil is dry, the seedlings can be left to shrivel up – but don't leave them if it's wet, in case they re-root.

Digging: Established weeds can be dug out with a garden fork, but it's sometimes difficult to remove those with vigorous root systems. Try using a Cape Cod weeder or fishtail weeder for single plants.

Weedkillers: Weedkillers are highly effective, but you should only use those that do not persist in the soil. Look for nonselective weedkillers containing glyphosate, which is relatively harmless to humans and animals once it has dried on the plant and leaves little residue in the soil. It is relatively fast acting and works extremely well.

Most weeds succumb to the first dose, although really vigorous types may need several applications.

Because glyphosate is nonselective, however, it will kill any plant that it somes in contact with – weeds and ornamentals alike. This is not a problem in large areas, such as a neglected bed overrun with weeds; here you can spray the whole patch, wait for the weeds to die

back completely, then prepare the soil and plant. If a tenacious weed is in the middle of the garden, however, you will need to spot treat carefully on a windless day, so that the spray will not drift onto desirable plants.

Loose mulches: Mulching with compost, well-rotted manure, shredded bark, or wood chips keeps down annual weeds and smothers perennials – a 3 in/7.5cm layer should be sufficient.

Sheet mulches: Impervious mulches such as black or clear plastic are invaluable for clearing large areas. Most perennial weeds will be completely smothered in one growing season, though more persistent types may need two. Black plastic can also be used in weed-infested borders and covered with a thin layer of soil or one of the loose mulches. A thick layer of newspaper can be used in the same way and will eventually rot into the soil. Alternatively, lay down permeable landscaping fabric when planting borders – it allows air and water to pass through but suppresses weeds.

Plants: It takes a thief to catch a thief – garden plants are the best and most decorative weed control of all, so plant as densely as you can, using a good proportion of ground covers. Once these plants are growing well, weeds are deprived of light and will be forced to give up the unequal struggle.

Stinging nettles

Top Ten Weeds

Groundsel

• BINDWEED (*Convolvulus*)
This perennial climber has white trumpet flowers and thick ropes of smooth, off-white roots which quickly colonize new areas, sending out further stems. Digging out the roots helps, but any overlooked portion will resprout. In large, uncultivated areas, spray with weedkiller or smother with black plastic. Where it is growing among garden plants, keep pulling up the stems or spot treat carefully with weedkiller.

• BRAMBLES
Though the blackberries may be tempting, brambles send out rooting runners and grow into substantial clumps if not controlled. Established plants are virtually impossible to dig out, so try starving them. Cut down the existing stems to ground level (wearing heavy gloves), then do the same to any ensuing growth. The effort of continually producing new shoots will exhaust the plant within a year. If you prefer to use weedkiller, you will probably have to make several applications.

• CHICKWEED
Chickweed forms a sprawling, low-growing mass of small leaves and tiny white flowers. This is a very persistent annual and should be hoed or hand-pulled as soon as you spot it.

• CRABGRASS
The creeping white roots send up stems of broad-leaved grass at regular intervals; any small portion of root can resprout. Can be controlled with a pre-emergent weedkiller.

• DANDELION
There are many varieties of this perennial, but all have the familiar yellow sun-ray flowers and rosettes of toothed leaves; the deep tap root is a real menace. Where it's impossible to dig it out (in paving or close to ornamental plants, for instance), apply a weedkiller to the young leaves. In lawns, spot treat with a selective broad-leaf weedkiller.

• DOCK
A perennial with long, lance-shaped leaves and tall plumes of rusty seedheads, sometimes as much as 3 ft/90cm high. The deep tap roots are very tenacious but can be eliminated in the same way as dandelions.

• GOUTWEED
This low-growing perennial has leaves and flowers that closely resemble those of the elder tree. Creeping underground stems send out an advancing army of shoots. Digging has some effect (though it will resprout from any pieces you miss), as does a mulch at least 4 in/10cm deep. Alternatively, treat the emerging spring leaves with weedkiller and repeat the operation in summer.

• GROUNDSEL
Groundsel is an annual that grows to around 1 ft/30cm with small yellow, thistle-shaped flowers. Hoe or hand weed, but if the plant is in flower,

Dandelions

IDEAS FOR LOW-MAINTENANCE

Careful grouting between bricks or paving stones will save you endless hours of weeding.

Don't worry too much about lawn weeds. Violets are pretty and clover is beneficial (it adds nitrogen). Anything more invasive can quickly be spot treated with a selective broad-leaf weedkiller that won't kill the grass.

Weeds that creep in from a neighboring garden can be a real menace. Some are so deep-rooted that there's little you can do. But for ground elder, creeping butter-cups, and nettles, a physical barrier (of thick plastic for instance) set in the ground to a depth of 18 in/45cm will keep them out.

WEEDING TIPS

Don't forget that annual weeds can ger-minate and set seed in mild spells in winter, so keep the hoe handy.

If you can't beat them, eat them. Goutweed can be cooked like spinach, nettles made into soup, and dandelion, bittercress, and chickweed leaves added to salads.

When applying weedkiller, follow the manufacturer's instructions to the letter and use on calm, still days.

UNDERSTANDING THE ENEMY

Weeds fall into two broad categories – annual nuisances and perennial pests. Annual weeds are shallow rooted and rely on the quick production of masses of seed to keep going, and some can raise several generations in a year. Fortunately, most are easy to hoe or hand-weed. Some common annual weeds are chickweed, crabgrass, and purslane.

Perennial weeds are a more diverse group, with several different means of causing trouble. Some form a deep taproot that clings tenaciously, and if the top of the root is snapped off, the remainder will usually resprout.

Others increase from long stems that root where they touch the ground or by sending up stems from creeping roots. Perennial weeds include Canada thistle, dandelion, ground ivy, brambles, plantain, and goutweed.

always break the stem – an intact plant has enough remaining energy to set seed even after you've put it on the compost heap.

◆ MUSTARDS

These annuals have lobed, cresslike leaves arranged in a rosette, heads of small yellow flowers, and long, narrow seedpods that explode when ripe. It's easy enough to hand pull or hoe, but try to catch it before the seeds are set.

◆ NETTLES

Hairy-leaved, stinging nettles are one of the easier perennials to get rid of (but be sure to wear gloves). The fibrous yellow roots creep and send up new stems, but they're shallow enough to dig up in their entirety. In awkward places where you can't dig, spray the patch with a glysophate weedkiller.

THE MOST FEARSOME WEEDS OF ALL

Horsetail

The most noxious thugs in the world of weeds are Japanese knotweed and horsetail (sometimes called mare's tail), though fortunately they're localized rather than widespread. Japanese knotweed forms great stands of pinkish bamboolike stems

and broad oval leaves, with loose sprays of white flowers, to a height of 8 ft/2.4m or more. Horsetail is a prehistoric plant that emerges something like an erect, dull green bottlebrush.

They're so vigorous that you need a good deal of persistence to get rid of them. The roots go so deep that digging is of no use at all, and pulling the tops off is a life sentence. If the invasion's not yet too serious, chemicals should work – crush the leaves and stems when plants are growing vigorously in summer and apply a weedkiller containing glyphosate. Several applications will probably

be needed. For more serious infestations, it's best to smother them. Laying sheets of black plastic or newspaper over the whole area will deprive them of light and will eventually kill them off, though it may take up to two years to eliminate them completely.

Japanese knotweed

The garden year

One of the greatest pleasures in gardening is that the garden changes continually throughout the year. After the starkness of winter, it slowly comes alive with delicate new growth in spring, turns lush with color and scent in summer, and blazes with color in fall before shifting again into a subtler, quieter mood.

Our job is to keep the garden looking its best year-round, no matter what the season. This requires planning, digging, planting, mulching, feeding, pruning, and weeding — but the more you put into gardening, the more you'll get out of it. Even tedious tasks will seem more bearable because of the beautiful surroundings and the pleasure of watching plants grow.

Beginning gardeners may feel overwhelmed at first, not knowing what to do or when to do it. While the preceding chapters covered many of the necessary techniques, the garden calendar that follows will help you with the timing. There are also some basic ideas you can use for planning your dream garden to be appealing throughout the year.

While reading through this section, it will be helpful to keep these points in mind:

• The calendar contains seasonal guidelines only — not hard-and-fast rules. Because the climate across the country is so diverse — as are the needs of individual plants — you will need to judge for yourself when the time is right to perform a particular task. Experience is the best teacher.
• Don't worry about doing a task late or forgetting it — plants can be remarkably forgiving. If you didn't get around to aerating the lawn in spring, do it in fall. If you neglected to clip back an azalea after it flowered one year, do it the next.
• Use common sense — gardening is not a mystery. If a container plant looks hot and wilted in intense summer sun, give it a drink or some shade.
• Some of the best gardening tips involve *not* doing something, such as not working wet soil. This is the easiest advice of all to follow.

YEAR-ROUND INTEREST

The first step in gardening is to ensure that the landscape will be appealing year-round, so plan for beauty in every season and within every season. When one plant has finished flowering, make sure there is another with blossoms or fruit to take its place. And when the whole garden slows down in fall, provide a variety of plants with evergreen foliage, bark, or other features to keep the landscape lively. The seasonal stars should be set against a good backdrop of leaf textures and plant shapes for contrast and structure.

SPRING SURPRISES

The first leaves of the daffodils and other spring bulbs pushing out of the soil announce the beginning of the garden year — it won't be long before the garden is bursting with color again.

Once the bulbs are well on their way, there's a succession of trees with exquisite flowers — from dogwoods *(Cornus)* and serviceberries *(Amelanchier)* to

Lavender will bring interest to your garden year-round.

*A densely planted strawberry jar brings cheerful
color to early summer.*

*A beautiful collection of pines gives the impression
of a mountain landscape.*

cherries (*Prunus*) and crab apples (*Malus*). Another good
bet for spring color are the magnolias, especially the
saucer magnolia (*Magnolia soulangeana*). These are
complemented by shrubs, including forsythia and lilacs
for sun and pieris, azaleas, and rhododendrons for
shade.

Don't forget perennials — creeping phlox,
pulmonaria, violets, and bleeding heart are among the
best for spring color. And if you have room for a climber,
plant *Clematis montana*, which blooms abundantly.

SUMMER SCENTS AND COLORS

Summer is the time for rich colors and heady perfumes
— made all the more intense by the blazing sun. Roses
are the undisputed champions of this season, for their
range of blossom shapes, colors, and scents. Many of the
older varieties have lovely fragrances, and the new
English roses (which combine the hardiness of shrub
roses with the ever-blooming flowers of modern hybrids)
are both fragrant and prolific. Other scented summer
bloomers include lilies — which come in a range of
colors, from deep rose to ice white — lavender,

flowering tobacco, wisteria, and honeysuckle.

Also look for plants that provide flowers over a long
period. Hardy geraniums bloom generously for a month
or more and will bloom again if cut back. Baby's breath
and lythrum will also repeat. Iris, poppies, and daylilies
on the other hand, are shorter-lived, but summer
wouldn't be the same without them.

Trees that bloom in summer are rarer than spring-
flowering types, but stewartia, crape myrtle, and
golden-rain tree all provide pretty blossoms. The same
holds true of shrubs; look for buddleia, cistus, and, of
course, hydrangea.

FALL FIRE

While a number of perennials bloom into fall —
including black-eyed Susan, asters, and Japanese
anemone — and some annuals, like impatiens, flower
until frost, fall is the season for foliage and fruits.

The entire maple family (*Acer*) and many cherries
(*Prunus*) put on brilliant displays of red, gold, and
orange leaves in fall. Just as beautiful, if sometimes
subtler, is the foliage of birches, dogwoods, beeches,

Crocosmia *(Montbretia) is one of the joys of late summer, easing the garden into fall.*

and oaks. Vines can be equally colorful: plant Virginia creeper or Boston ivy against your house, and their bright crimson leaves will seem to set the walls on fire.

When it comes to fruits, nothing beats the crab apples, whose red or golden fruits glisten through the season and often into winter. Also look for hollies and mountain ash, which produce large crops of berries, and for the wall shrub pyracantha.

WINTER PLEASURES

In winter you'll need to be more creative to keep the landscape interesting, but there are still plenty of options. This is the time when evergreens — including trees, shrubs, or some perennials — really shine, all the more so if the foliage is variegated with white or gold. Hemlock, spruce, cedar, and pine, along with hollies, rhododendron, and boxwood, are all good choices.

Ornamental bark and branch structure can also add beauty. The white stems of birches, the mottled bark of eucalyptus, and the satiny trunk of the Sargent cherry can all be best appreciated when the landscape is relatively bare. Red- and yellow-twig dogwoods glow against the snow, while the weeping branches of

Harvest time in the gardening year.

certain willows and the soaring limbs of the sycamore will float like sculptures against the sky.

There are flowering plants for winter, in both warm and cold climates. Favorites for mild areas are winter jasmine, camellia, *Mahonia lomariifolia,* and *Viburnum tinus.* In cold regions, you can plant winter hazel, witch hazel, or the Christmas rose *(Helleborus niger).*

MIDWINTER

Trees and Shrubs

• After heavy snow, gently brush accumulated snow from plants to prevent damage to the branches. Also check for rodent damage and protect bark with wire mesh.

• Check plants for any broken stems and prune them off; otherwise, they might be torn off in strong wind.

• Take a good look at your garden in the "down" season — if it lacks appeal, plan to add some plants that offer winter interest.

• Examine plants for dead, diseased, or awkwardly placed branches — this is the best time to view the plant's structure — and note those that will need pruning later in the year.

• Check on roses to make sure their winter protection is adequate.

• Make sure tools are ready for the season; repair or replace them as needed.

Flowers

• Check the garden periodically to see if perennials have been heaved out of the soil by frost. If so, press them back in place gently and heap on some extra mulch.

• Read seed catalogs and select varieties for the coming year.

• Check any stored bulbs and discard those that have rotted.

• Make sure gardening tools are ready for the season — with blades sharpened, joints oiled, and handles secure. Repair or replace them as needed.

Lawns

• Don't use salt to melt snow on paved areas near the lawn, as runoff can damage the grass.

• Get the mower ready for spring. Sharpen the blades and bring the mower to a repair shop if it needs to be serviced.

Kitchen Gardens

• Read catalogs and select seeds and plants for the coming year.

Container Gardens

• Check plants overwintering indoors; make sure they are getting the necessary amount of light and their location remains cool and dry.

• Water plants in containers only if the soil is very dry.

Arrange containers together, and they will protect each other.

• In cold areas, check that outdoor plants have sufficient winter protection and add more if necessary.

• In warm areas, protect tender plants from cold weather by draping them with floating row covers.

• Shop for new containers; garden centers often have winter sales and you can pick up some bargains. Also stock up on potting soil.

Water Gardening

• If there are fish in the pond, the water should not be allowed to freeze over. Melt a hole in the ice along the edge by setting a pan of hot water on the surface; repeat as needed.

• Look through catalogs from growers specializing in water plants and select new specimens.

Houseplants

• Don't overwater plants — let the soil dry out between waterings.

• Keep plants out of drafts and move them off windowsills at night if they can't tolerate cold temperatures.

LATE WINTER

Trees and Shrubs
- Once the soil is workable, plant and transplant trees and shrubs.
- Remove staking from trees that were planted the previous winter.
- Remove burlap screens or other winter protection.
- Remove dead plants. It's easier to cut them down when there is no foliage, and tree surgeons often have lower rates in the off-season.
- If you want to stimulate vigorous growth, prune plants while they are still dormant, before growth begins.
- Cut back summer-flowering shrubs, such as some hydrangeas, if needed. Also cut back shrubs with colorful stems, such as red-twig dogwoods.
- Check any ties on staked trees that had been planted last fall and loosen if necessary to allow for growth in the coming year.
- Spray dormant-oil pesticide on plants to kill overwintering insects.
- Have the soil tested around plants and add lime or sulfur to adjust the pH.
- Order plants from catalogs or place special orders with nurseries.

Flowers
- Plan any design changes so you will be ready to plant in early spring.
- Order plants and seeds from catalogs.
- Cut back any perennials that you had left for winter interest and clean up any winter debris from the beds; be careful not to step on plant crowns when walking in the beds.
- When the soil is workable, prepare empty beds with lime, organic matter, or other amendments as needed so that the ground will be ready for planting time. But be patient: don't try to work cold, wet soil — it will just become compacted.
- In cold areas, sow seeds of slow-growing annuals indoors, so they will be ready to plant outdoors once danger of frost has passed.
- In warm areas, sow seed and plant cold-tolerant annuals such as pansies. Also plant hardy summer-flowering bulbs outdoors.
- Watch for the early bulbs, such as winter aconite and snowdrop, to begin emerging.

Lawns
- As weather permits, have a soil sample tested and add amendments, such as lime, if needed.
- Check on lawn supplies, such as seed and fertilizer, and stock up as needed.
- Walk over the lawn and look carefully for signs of fungal diseases that develop in winter.
- Note where water collects from snow melt or rain and correct the grade level with topsoil when the ground is dry.

Kitchen Gardens
- Map out your garden on paper — being sure to rotate vegetable crops to different locations from the previous year — and make a planting schedule.
- In cold areas, warm up vegetable beds by stretching black plastic mulch over the soil and securing the edges with stones.
- When the soil is workable, dig organic matter into empty vegetable beds so that the amendments will break down before planting time.
- In cold areas, start onion seeds and seed potatoes indoors.
- In mild areas, plant potatoes, peppers, and warm-season crops such as squash outdoors.
- Cut back fall-fruiting raspberry canes to ground level.
- Clean up any winter debris from herb gardens.

Container Gardens
- Cut or pinch back any plants overwintered indoors that have become leggy.
- Begin increasing water and fertilizer of plants overwintered indoors to stimulate growth.
- In warm areas, plant cool-season annuals, such as pansies, and summer-flowering bulbs in pots outdoors.

Water Gardens
- Continue as on page 144.

Houseplants
- Continue to water plants lightly.
- Wipe off leaves (except those of fuzzy- or spiny-leaved plants) with a damp cloth.
- Make sure windows are sparkling clean to maximize the amount of light admitted.

EARLY SPRING

Trees and Shrubs

* Once the soil is workable, plant and transplant trees and shrubs if you have not done so earlier.
* Fertilize all plants with a balanced food, such as 10-10-10 for trees and 5-10-10 for shrubs.
* Remove staking from trees that were planted the previous spring.
* Cut back honeysuckle and other vigorous climbers hard if they have become overgrown.

Flowers

* Prepare empty beds with lime, organic matter, or other amendments as needed if you haven't done so earlier.
* In cold areas, plant cold-tolerant annuals, such as pansies, outdoors.
* Sow seed of fast-growing annuals indoors so that you can plant them out after danger of frost has passed.
* In warm areas, plant out warm-weather annuals.
* Feed perennials with a balanced fertilizer such as 5-10-5 and spread a ring of compost around them.
* In warm areas, transplant or divide and replant perennials if you haven't done it the previous fall.
* Feed spring-flowering bulbs with a high-phosphorus fertilizer, such as bonemeal or 5-10-10.
* In cold areas, plant hardy summer-flowering bulbs.

Lawns

* Rake the grass vigorously to clean up leaves, dead grass, and other debris.
* Aerate the lawn to promote good drainage.
* Apply a slow-release organic fertilizer formulated for blade growth.
* Overseed the lawn if needed. If the weather is dry, mist the new seeds to keep them moist until they germinate.
* Seed or sod new lawns or repair bare patches as soon as weather permits.
* In heavy soil, spread gypsum (calcium sulfate) to help "open" the soil to water, air, and nutrients.
* Mow the lawn once growth begins. To stimulate blade growth, cut the grass a bit shorter than usual the first few times, then adjust the blade to cut at the highest recommended height for the grass variety.

Kitchen Gardens

* In cold areas, sow cold-tolerant vegetables such as lettuce and radishes outdoors when weather permits; sow every 2–4 weeks so that you can harvest continually. Sow seeds for early tomato varieties indoors.
* In cold areas, plant onion sets and potatoes outdoors once the soil is workable.
* In warm areas, continue planting warm-weather vegetables outdoors.
* Feed established herbs very lightly with a balanced fertilizer.

Container Gardens

* Fertilize outdoor potted plants as soon as the soil has thawed.
* Set out any pots of spring-flowering bulbs that have overwintered indoors.
* In cold areas, plant cool-season annuals, such as pansies, and summer-flowering bulbs in pots outdoors.
* Prune containerized trees and shrubs that may have become overgrown.
* Transplant any containerized trees or shrubs into larger pots if necessary. Alternatively, you can remove and replace the top 4–6in/10–15cm of soil.

Water Gardens

* Start to feed the fish in an established pond as the weather warms and they become more active.
* Install a new pond so that the water will be able to settle before planting time.

Houseplants

* Gradually increase watering.
* Begin fertilizing when new growth appears.
* Repot plants into large containers as needed.

Tulips and daffodils are the essence of early spring.

MIDSPRING

Trees and Shrubs

+ Fertilize all plants with a balanced food, if you haven't done so earlier in the season.
+ Replenish permanent organic mulch around plants.
+ Remove staking from trees that have been in the ground for a year if you have not done so earlier.
+ Prune spring-flowering shrubs, such as forsythia, lilac, azalea, and jasmine, after they have bloomed.
+ Remove any winter mulch from roses so that the soil can warm up and dry out. Also remove any burlap screens or other winter protection.
+ Prune established roses, except climbers, to remove dead and weak stems and fertilize.
+ Plant new roses.

Flowers

+ Purchase perennials from nurseries and plant as weather permits.
+ In cold areas, transplant or divide and replant perennials as needed.
+ Replenish the organic mulch in established perennial beds to help suppress weeds, keep roots cool, and retain moisture.
+ Sow seeds of hardy annuals, such as pot marigold and California poppy, outdoors.
+ Deadhead any bulbs that have finished flowering but let the foliage die back naturally.
+ In warm areas, plant tender summer-flowering bulbs outdoors, including cannas and dahlias.
+ Apply a pre-emergent herbicide in beds only if annual weeds have been a problem.
+ In warm areas, watch for signs of pests and diseases and treat as needed.

Lawns

+ Aerate the lawn, and overseed as needed, if you have not done so earlier in the season.
+ Apply a pre-emergent herbicide for crabgrass, but keep it away from trees and shrubs.
+ Keep newly seeded or sodded lawns well watered until they are established but do not overwater.
+ Continue mowing the grass to the highest recommended height for the grass variety.
+ In warm areas, watch for fungal diseases and signs of pest damage.

Kitchen Gardens

+ In cold areas, plant out beets and members of the broccoli family *(Brassica)*.
+ Harvest perennial vegetables such as asparagus as they come into season.
+ Continue sowing cold-tolerant vegetables every 2–4 weeks until it gets warm.
+ Thin vegetable seedlings so that the plants don't get overcrowded; you can eat the thinnings as baby vegetables.
+ In cold areas, start the rest of the tomato seeds indoors and transplant your seedlings of early varieties into larger pots, to give them room to grow.
+ In warm areas, plant out more hot-weather vegetables such as okra.
+ In warm areas, give heavy feeders like peppers and tomatoes a boost with all-purpose fertilizer.
+ Trim back lavender cotton to promote bushiness.

Container Gardens

+ In cold areas, start tender plants for containers indoors so you will have established specimens for outdoor pots and baskets as soon as weather permits.
+ Watch the weather forecast and protect any outdoor plants if frost threatens.
+ In warm areas, water and feed plants as needed and watch for signs of pests or diseases. Deadhead spent blooms to promote long flowering and pinch back new growth to prevent legginess.
+ In warm areas, replace any spent cool-season annuals with warm-weather specimens, such as marigold, impatiens and zinnias.

Water Gardens

+ Start planting in your pond.
+ Lift and divide overgrown plants but do not divide iris and marsh marigold until after they have flowered.
+ Clear algae as needed. You can remove weedy types by twirling them around a stick and lifting them from the water.

Houseplants

+ Begin watering cacti and move them to a warm, bright location.
+ Take cuttings if you want to propagate plants.

LATE SPRING

Trees and Shrubs
- Prune plants if you want to reduce their overall size.
- Replenish permanent organic mulch around plants if you haven't done so earlier in the season.
- Watch for pests and diseases and treat as needed.
- After you have enjoyed the abundance of flowers, deadhead the plants as soon as possible.
- Watch for suckers and water sprouts and snap them off at their bases, where they meet the main stem.
- Fertilize established roses and watch for signs of pests and diseases. Water if the weather is dry.

Flowers
- In cold areas, plant out tender annuals and summer-flowering bulbs as soon as all danger of frost has passed.
- When replacing cool-weather annuals with warm-weather types, replenish the soil with organic matter or other amendments.
- Continue to deadhead annuals for repeat blooms.
- Sow perennials seeds outdoors for flowering plants the following year.
- Deadhead perennials to prevent them from setting seed (unless you want to collect it) and perhaps to encourage a second bloom.
- Stake peonies plants before they bloom, so they will not fall over once the heavy flower heads form.
- Monitor for weeds and signs of pests and diseases.

Lawns
- Continue mowing the lawn at the highest recommended height for the grass variety.
- Apply broad-leaf weed control if weeds have been a persistent problem.
- Spot treat or remove by hand individual weeds.

Kitchen Gardens
- In cold areas, sow seed outdoors for warm-weather crops such as beans; sow every 2–4 weeks if you want to harvest continually.
- Once all danger of frost has passed, plant out vegetable seedlings that you started indoors. Cover with floating row covers if late frost threatens.
- In cold areas, plant some of the tomato seedlings outdoors late in the season, but watch for late frosts. Also start some late tomato varieties indoors.
- Continue to thin seedlings.
- Draw up soil in a mound over potatoes to keep them covered.
- Keep vegetables well watered in dry weather.
- Monitor and treat vegetables for pests and diseases.
- Weed religiously, as weeds rob water and nutrients from vegetables. Use an organic or inorganic mulch to suppress weeds.
- Shear back thyme after it has flowered to keep it compact and deadhead lamb's ears.
- Plant basil after all danger of frost has passed.

Container Gardens
- Set out tender plants that have overwintered indoors as soon as all danger of frost has passed.
- Water plants as needed, mulching the soil to retain moisture.
- Watch for pests and diseases.
- Deadhead spent blooms.

Water Gardens
- Continue adding plants if desired.

Houseplants
- Continue watering and feeding regularly.
- Buy new plants from the garden center.

Late spring is a good time to purchase new houseplants from the garden center.

EARLY SUMMER

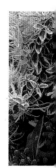

Trees and Shrubs

- Prune hedges for shape and bushiness.
- If certain plants are vulnerable to mildew in humid weather, thin them out lightly to increase air circulation.
- Continue to water any new plants until they are established.
- Spray plants with a strong jet of water throughout summer to dislodge pests and dust.
- Monitor all plants for pests and diseases and treat as needed.
- Enlarge the mulch ring around specimen plants if the canopy has outgrown it.
- Watch for shoots on variegated plants that have reverted and cut them back to their base.
- Check evergreens for yellowing leaves and spray with a high-nitrogen foliar food if needed.
- Give rhododendron and other broad-leaf evergreens a boost with a light feeding of high-phosphorus fertilizer.
- Prune ever-blooming climbing roses to perpetuate bloom and prune spring-blooming climbers after they have bloomed.
- Deadhead spent rose blooms and fertilize, water, and mulch the plants. Watch for pests and diseases and treat as needed.

Flowers

- Sow seeds of warm-weather annuals like zinnias outdoors.
- After the spring flush of flowers has passed, examine the garden for bare spots and fill in with annuals for the short term or with perennials for the following year.
- Continue to deadhead all flowering plants.
- Water if the weather is very hot and dry. In arid areas, make sure you have mulched all beds well to conserve moisture.
- Continue to watch for pests and diseases and treat as needed.
- Start seeds for specimens you want to plant out in fall.
- Snip off the foliage of spring bulbs after it has yellowed and withered completely.

Lawns

- Continue mowing the grass at the highest recommended height for the grass variety.
- Water only if the weather has been very hot and dry,

providing 1in/2.5cm of water per week.
- Watch for weeds, pests, and diseases and treat as needed.

Kitchen Gardens

- Sow seeds for vegetables you want to set out in fall.
- Give heavy feeders, like tomatoes and corn, a boost of all-purpose fertilizer if you haven't done it earlier in the season.
- Let perennial vegetables like asparagus go to seed.
- Monitor for pests and diseases and treat as needed.
- Harvest vegetables early in the morning when possible.
- In cold areas, set out all the remaining tomato seedlings and remove any frost protection from plants that are already outdoors.
- Stake and train vining tomatoes, pole beans, and squash.
- Clean up any young apples and pears that have fallen, but don't panic — this early-season "drop" is normal.
- Keep raspberries well watered while fruit is developing.
- Cut back lavender after it has flowered to keep it compact.

Container Gardens

- Continue monitoring plants for moisture stress and water as needed.
- Feed with a dilute fertilizer once a month throughout summer.
- Pinch back leggy plants and deadhead spent blooms religiously.

Water Gardens

- Visit garden centers that sell water plants so you can view the plants in full leaf and, sometimes, in flower.
- Watch for aphids on water plants and spray them with a jet of water. If there are fish in the pond, lay a piece of fine mesh over the affected plants to sink them slightly and fish will eat the insects.

Houseplants

- Continue watering and feeding regularly.
- Set out tender houseplants for the summer but be sure to provide them with some shelter and do not let them bake in hot sun.
- Monitor plants for pests and treat as needed.

MIDSUMMER

Trees and Shrubs

- If the summer has been very wet, feed new plants lightly to replenish nutrients that have been washed away.
- Watch for pests and diseases and treat as needed.
- Continue watering new specimens if the weather is hot and dry and water established plants if there is a prolonged dry spell.
- Continue watering and feeding roses and watching for pests and diseases.
- Monitor climbing plants that are not self-clinging and tie them into supports or secure them to a wall with plant nails as needed.

Flowers

- Continue deadheading flowers. Also look for any stems that may have been broken and cut them off.
- Continue monitoring for pests and diseases.
- Water during prolonged dry spells.
- Look through catalogs for spring-flowering bulbs and place your orders for fall planting.
- Monitor summer-flowering bulbs and make sure they have enough food and water. Also stake them as needed to keep the heavy flower heads from bending the stems.

Lawns

- Make sure the mower blades remain sharp and sharpen if needed. A grayish cast to the lawn and frayed grass ends usually means the blades are dull.
- Water only in prolonged dry spells if there is no water ban; grass is resilient and can go dormant without harm.
- Watch for fungal diseases that spread in humid weather.

Kitchen Gardens

- Continue harvesting vegetables early in the morning. Be sure to check under leaves for ripening fruits.
- Clean up promptly any vegetables that have fallen and are inedible.
- Continue watering, weeding, and monitoring vegetables for pests and diseases as needed.
- In hot areas, use floating row covers to protect vegetables from heat and make sure there is sufficient mulch to retain moisture.
- Continue to train vining vegetables, like squash and tomatoes.

- Water fruit trees deeply if the weather has been hot and dry.
- Cut lemon balm back hard to keep it bushy; it will regrow quickly.

Container Gardens

- Continue watering and fertilizing.
- Continue pinching back leggy plants and deadheading.
- Continue watching for pests and diseases.

Water Gardens

- Deadhead flowers to prevent them from setting seed.
- Thin out any water lily leaves and oxygenating plants if they have become overcrowded.
- In extremely hot weather, aerate the pond to replenish lost oxygen by spraying it with a hose or turning on a fountain.
- Check the pond for water loss and refill as needed.

Houseplants

- Move plants, except for cacti and succulents, off of south-facing windowsills, which can be too hot in summer.
- If the weather is very dry, provide extra moisture by standing plants in gravel-filled trays or saucers that are filled with water to just below the base of the pots. Add more water as needed.

One of the gardening joys of summer are lush hanging baskets.

LATE SUMMER

Trees and Shrubs
- Plant evergreen trees and shrubs now, when they are dormant.
- Do not prune any plants and stop clipping hedges — they can still send out new growth, which would be killed in winter.
- Monitor plants that produce berries and keep them well watered to ensure the showiest crop.
- Stop fertilizing roses, as food could stimulate growth that would be killed in winter, but continue watering and treating for pests and diseases.

Flowers
- Cut back tired annuals and give them a boost with an all-purpose fertilizer — many will spring back for late-season bloom.
- Remove any annuals that are completely spent and replace them with fall plants, such as chrysanthemums, ornamental cabbages, or pansies.
- Continue watering, weeding, deadheading, and monitoring for pests and diseases.
- Make plans for planting perennials in fall and order plants from catalogs.
- Divide daylilies after they have finished blooming, making sure each piece has one or more growth buds.
- Plant Madonna lily bulbs and bulbs for fall-flowering crocus.

Lawns
- Continue mowing, but raise the blades about ½ in/1cm to begin stimulating root growth.
- If beetles were a problem earlier in summer, apply beneficial nematodes or another grub control to the lawn, where the grubs develop.
- Note bare spots that should be seeded in fall.

Kitchen Gardens
- Continue to harvest vegetables.
- Lift onions from the soil with a fork and let them ripen right on the ground if the weather is dry.
- Begin sowing seed of cool-weather vegetables for fall crops.
- Continue watering, weeding, and monitoring vegetables for pests and diseases. Clean up any fallen vegetables.

Summer means lots of hard work in the garden — but the result is worth it.

- Remove and compost any vegetable plants that have finished bearing fruit.
- Use fine-mesh plastic netting to keep birds away from ripening tomatoes and other fruits.
- Cut back the flowers of garlic chives before they set seed to prevent them from self-sowing.
- Dig up and pot any tender herbs you want to overwinter indoors, such as scented geraniums and rosemary.

Container Gardens
- Continue watering and fertilizing.
- Continue pinching back leggy plants and deadheading.
- Continue watching for pests and diseases.
- Replace any spent annuals with fall specimens, such as chrysanthemums, ornamental cabbage, or pansies.

Water Gardens
- Continue deadheading plants as needed.
- Continue aerating and refilling the pond as needed.

Houseplants
- Continue watering and fertilizing.
- Monitor for pests and treat as needed.
- Wipe off leaves (except those of fuzzy- or spiny-leaved plants) with a damp cloth.
- Repot any plants that have outgrown their containers.

EARLY FALL

Trees and Shrubs
• Plant or transplant container-grown or balled-and-burlapped specimens.
• Remove any staking from plants installed the previous fall.
• Clean up any debris from around plants and put in the compost.
• Continue watering roses and treating for pests and diseases.

Flowers
• Continue watering until plants are killed by frost and continue weeding.
• Take cuttings from any annuals you want to propagate indoors during the winter.
• Dig up and pot any tender plants you want to overwinter indoors.
• In cold areas, divide any perennials that have become thin in the middle or are crowding their neighbors.
• Collect seeds from any perennials that you want to propagate indoors over the winter.
• Cut back almost to ground level any perennials that you do not want to leave standing for winter interest. Sedums, for instance, are often left for their beauty and for their seeds, which attract birds.
• Set out in the garden any seedlings that you had started for fall planting.
• Plant spring-flowering bulbs.

Lawns
• Aerate the lawn if you did not do so in spring.
• Apply a slow-release organic fertilizer formulated for root growth.
• Have the soil tested and add amendments, such as lime, if you did not do so earlier in the year.
• Overseed the lawn or reseed bare patches if needed.
• Spread a thin layer — about ¼ in/6mm — of screened compost over the entire lawn.
• Apply broad-leaf weed control if weeds have been a problem, but keep it away from trees and shrubs.
• Continue mowing as needed, with the mower set ½ in/1cm higher than usual.

Kitchen Gardens
• Set out fall crops of cool-weather vegetables such as lettuce and broccoli.
• Keep an eye on tender vegetables, such as squash and tomatoes, if frost threatens and cover with a floating row cover.
• If a hard freeze threatens tender vegetables, harvest them all at once and store them indoors to ripen. Some vegetables, such as tomatoes, can also be used while still green.
• Don't worry about cold-hardy vegetables such as carrots and cabbage. The cold makes them produce extra sugars, and they will taste even better.
• Harvest any late peas but leave the roots in the ground — they will add nitrogen to the soil as they decompose.
• Dig up and compost any vegetables that have finished fruiting and clean up debris, which can harbor pests and diseases.
• Cut back to ground level the canes of summer-fruiting raspberries and of blackberries.

Container Gardens
• If frost threatens, cover plants with a floating row cover or old sheet or move them indoors.
• In warm climates, continue watering, feeding, deadheading, and monitoring for pests and diseases.
• Plant spring-flowering bulbs in containers for bloom the next year.
• Take cuttings of any plants you want to propagate indoors over the winter.

Water Gardens
• Spread a fine-mesh screen over the pond surface to catch falling leaves and debris; empty the contents into the compost regularly. Or skim out debris with a net.
• If the pond does not have fish and a lot of organic debris has accumulated, you can drain, clean, and refill it.
• Stop feeding fish once the temperature falls below 50°F/10°C.

Houseplants
• Begin reducing the amount of water you give plants and stop feeding by midfall.
• Bring in any plants that have spent the summer outdoors but check them very carefully for pests and diseases and treat if needed before reintroducing them indoors.

MIDFALL

Trees and Shrubs

◆ Spray evergreens with an antidessicant (available at garden centers) to help reduce moisture loss from the leaves during winter.

◆ Prune back any damaged or diseased branches.

◆ Make sure staking on young trees is secure but not too tight so that the plant can bend with the wind over winter.

◆ Keep plants well watered until the ground freezes hard so that the roots will have plenty of moisture.

◆ Clean up fallen leaves and debris around plants to keep pests and diseases from overwintering in the garden.

◆ Continue watering roses to prepare them for winter and treat for pests as needed.

Flowers

◆ Clean up and compost any annuals that have been killed back by frost.

◆ In warm climates, sow annual seeds for winter and early spring flowers.

◆ Feed perennials lightly with a balanced fertilizer and spread a layer of compost around them.

◆ Clean up all debris from the flower beds — it's a haven for insects and diseases.

◆ Replenish any permanent ornamental mulch that was washed or blown away during the growing season.

◆ Dig up any tender bulbs, such as cannas and dahlias, and store in a cool, dry place until next year.

Lawns

◆ Rake up fallen leaves completely — they will smother and damage grass if left on the lawn. Put them in the compost pile or stack them to rot into leaf mold.

◆ Continue mowing as needed, with the blade set ½ in/1cm higher than usual. In cold areas, cool-season grasses will continue to grow well into early winter.

Kitchen Gardens

◆ In cold climates, harvest carrots, parsnips, and other late crops.

◆ Carefully store winter squash, onions, and potatoes so that their skins do not get bruised (which can allow rot).

◆ In warm climates, plant cool-weather crops such as lettuce and broccoli.

◆ Thoroughly clean any vines and foliage from trellises and other supports and put in the compost. Remove,

Midfall is the time for deep color in the garden.

clean, and store the supports.

◆ Clean up and destroy any diseased apples or pears.

Container Gardens

◆ Clean up any annuals killed by frost and dump them along with the soil from the pots into the compost.

◆ Bring in any tender plants that you want to overwinter.

◆ To protect a large container plant from winter damage, cover the entire plant in a crate or box that has no top or bottom and fill loosely with straw or chopped leaves.

◆ Plunge containers of perennials into an unused area of the garden bed to protect them. You can also bury them in a trench filled with sand.

◆ In warm climates, plant cool-weather annuals such as pansies and pot marigolds in containers for winter color.

Water Gardens

◆ Continue cleaning leaves and debris out of the pond.

◆ Cut back the top growth of marginal plants and remove dead leaves from water lilies.

Houseplants

◆ Reduce watering, letting the soil dry out. Feed only those plants that are in flower.

◆ If your house is dry during the heating season, use portable humidifiers to increase moisture. Also stand plants in gravel-filled trays or saucers filled with water to just below the base of the pots; add more water as needed.

◆ Gradually stop watering cacti and keep them dry in a cool location. Water lightly if they begin to wither.

LATE FALL

Trees and Shrubs

- In snowy areas, protect upright evergreens from damage by wrapping rope diagonally around the plant from top to bottom to compress the branches against the trunk.
- Protect shrubs from winter damage with a screen made from burlap sheets stretched around four stakes. For extra insulation around deciduous plants, loosely fill the interior with straw or chopped leaves.
- Watch for damage from mice or other rodents around tree trunks. If the bark has been nibbled, pull the mulch away from the base and wrap the trunk in a plastic sleeve with small ventilation holes or a fine-mesh wire screen.
- Wrap the trunks of young trees with paper tree wrap to prevent sunscald and wind burn.
- Continue watering plants until the ground freezes.
- Cover with evergreen boughs any small shrubs vulnerable to wind or sun damage.
- Mound up to 12in/30cm of soil or mulch around the base of rose bushes to protect the graft union from frost.
- Clean, oil, and store garden tools you have finished using.

Flowers

- Prepare new beds for planting in spring by turning over the soil, working in organic matter, then letting it lie — frost will break up any clumps, and your work will be easier in spring.
- In warm areas, protect tender plants from late frost by draping them with floating row covers. Clean up any spent plants and compost them.
- In warm areas, divide any perennials that have become thin in the middle or are crowding their neighbors.
- Make sure newly planted bulbs have adequate water and mulch protection and are marked with weatherproof labels.
- In cold areas, take in hoses and watering cans; check for cracks or leaks and repair or replace. Clean, oil, and store garden tools. Remove any stakes or other supports from

Robinias and maples provide beautiful, mellow fall color.

the garden, clean, and store till next year.

Lawns

- Continue mowing as needed.
- In warm climates, water the lawn deeply if the weather has been dry.

Kitchen Gardens

- Prepare new vegetable beds for planting in spring by turning over the soil roughly, working in organic matter, then letting it lie — frost will break up any clumps, and your work will be easier in spring.
- Add mulch around perennial vegetables such as asparagus.
- In warm climates, tend fall vegetable crops to ensure a good yield. If frost threatens, drape plants with a floating row cover.
- In warm climates, plant strawberries.
- Cut back the spent top growth from herbs and clean up leaves and debris from the bed. Do not cut back French tarragon until the top has been killed by a hard frost.

Container Gardens

- Keep remaining plants well watered until the soil freezes.
- Plant hardy dwarf evergreen shrubs in pots for winter interest.
- In warm climates, continue watering, fertilizing, and monitoring for signs of pests and diseases.

Water Gardens

- Continue removing debris as needed.

Houseplants

- Continue to water lightly; let tap water reach room temperature before watering plants. Continue providing extra humidity.
- Feed only flowering plants, such as cyclamen and poinsettias.
- Try to keep plants at an even temperature and keep them out of cold drafts.
- Move plants to locations with the most light.

EARLY WINTER

Trees and Shrubs

• Replenish any permanent ornamental mulch that has been blown or washed away.

• Lightly clip hollies, spruces, and other evergreens for holiday decoration if desired but do not do major pruning.

• Continue to check for rodent damage around tree trunks and provide protection.

• Continue watering plants until the soil freezes hard.

• Check on young roses and press them gently back into the ground if they have been heaved up by frost. Make sure they have 12in/30cm of mulch mounded up around the bases.

• Drape young ground-cover roses with evergreen boughs or floating row covers for protection. Cover climbing roses with burlap to shield them from wind.

• Ask nurseries for hard-to-find specimens you want to add to the garden; they may be able to order them from specialty growers.

Flowers

• In cold climates, make sure the garden is completely cleaned up before snow falls.

• In warm climates, continue deadheading and watering annuals and perennials and cut back and clean up any plants that have faded. Provide protection with a floating row cover if cold weather threatens.

• Continue watering newly planted bulbs if the weather is dry and check on mulch protection.

Lawns

• In cold climates, make sure you have cleared away all the leaves before snow falls.

• If you have finished cutting the grass for the year, clean off and store the lawn mower (with the gas tank drained).

• In warm climates, treat the lawn with a broad-leaf herbicide if weeds have been a problem, but keep it away from trees and shrubs.

Kitchen Gardens

• Check on stored vegetables and throw away any that have spoiled.

• In warm areas, harvest any late vegetable crops.

• In warm areas, protect tender herbs from frost by draping them with a floating row cover.

Aim to include some hardy evergreens in the garden.

Container Gardens

• Continue watering plants until the soil freezes.

• In warm climates, continue watering, fertilizing, and monitoring for signs of pests and diseases.

• Clean and store any containers that you have finished using for the year.

Water Gardens

• Prevent ice damage to the pond liner by floating several empty, sealed plastic bottles, with weights tied to their necks, in the water; you can also use logs or large rubber balls. The ice will press against the bottles instead of the liner.

• Because fish become lethargic in cold weather and are more vulnerable to predators, put a length of drain pipe in the bottom of the pond so they have a hiding place.

Houseplants

• Continue watering lightly with room-temperature water and providing extra humidity.

• Continue feeding flowering plants.

Temperature Zone Map

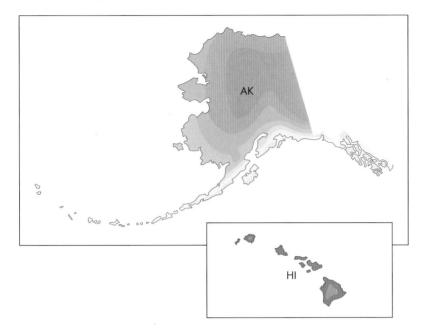

Selecting plants that are adapted to your climate is half the secret of successful gardening. You probably already know where the warm and cold spots in your garden are, but if you've just moved in, and want to know which plants will survive, and where, a zone map is a very useful aid. A plant that is well suited to its surroundings will flourish with a minimum of help, while a plant transplanted to an inhospitable site will struggle no matter how much care you give it.

TEMPERATURES ACROSS THE COUNTRY

This map is an adaptation of the standard US Department of Agriculture Plant Hardiness Zone Map, which is widely used in gardening books, magazines, and plant catalogs. It shows the average minimum temperatures across the country. It divides Canada and the United States, including the Hawaiian Islands, into 11 zones. Most American and Canadian nurseries and mail-order companies have adopted the USDA map as a reference.

The average minimum temperature is an index of the local winter's severity. In most cases this temperature is the crucial factor in determining whether a plant will survive in a given region.

Obviously, climates change, and overlap, so the lines of separation are not as clear cut as implied here. In the Best Plants sections, we have noted which plants are hardy in which zones, but don't feel that you have to restrict yourself too rigidly. Many plants recommended for one zone will likely do well in the southern part of the adjoining colder zone; they will also succeed in the adjoining warmer zones.

TEMPERATURES IN YOUR GARDEN

The other thing to bear in mind, is that your garden has its own variety of temperatures. For a start, temperature varies considerably with height. A garden located at the

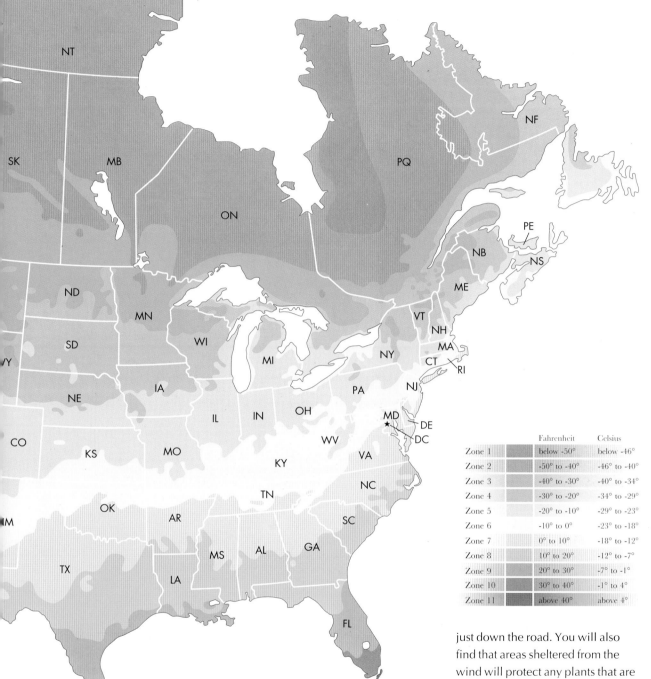

		Fahrenheit	Celsius
Zone 1		below -50°	below -46°
Zone 2		-50° to -40°	-46° to -40°
Zone 3		-40° to -30°	-40° to -34°
Zone 4		-30° to -20°	-34° to -29°
Zone 5		-20° to -10°	-29° to -23°
Zone 6		-10° to 0°	-23° to -18°
Zone 7		0° to 10°	-18° to -12°
Zone 8		10° to 20°	-12° to -7°
Zone 9		20° to 30°	-7° to -1°
Zone 10		30° to 40°	-1° to 4°
Zone 11		above 40°	above 4°

top of a 1,000 ft/300 m mountain, for example, will usually have temperatures several degrees colder than one in the surrounding plains. Thus any high spots in your garden will be cooler than elsewhere. In addition, a south-facing wall, and the surrounding area, will be warmer than that of a north-facing wall. And because water collects heat from the sun, a garden that is located on the shore of the pond will be warmer in winter; it will also be cooler in summer than in a garden just down the road. You will also find that areas sheltered from the wind will protect any plants that are marginally hardy.

Such local peculiarities and microclimates may force an adjustment in your use of the temperature zone map. If you have further questions about plant hardiness in your area, contact your local Cooperative Extension or Agricultural Service.

Index

GARDEN NOTES

Garden Notes